Without the voice of co̶n̶d̶e̶m̶n̶a̶t̶i̶o̶n̶, D̶r̶. G̶e̶r̶h̶a̶r̶t̶ gives us valuable wisdom and practical tools for our daily struggles with sin. As I read his insightful book, I found myself frequently saying, "I didn't know that!" Now I often quote him in my presentations and watch as others experience that *Aha!* moment. Don't be deceived; you need to read this book.

—GEORGIA SHAFFER
PROFESSIONAL SPEAKER, LEADERSHIP COACH, PA LICENSED PSYCHOLOGIST, AUTHOR OF *A GIFT OF MOURNING GLORIES: RESTORING YOUR LIFE AFTER LOSS*, AND PRODUCER OF THE SYNDICATED RADIO FEATURE *THE MOURNING GLORY MINUTE*

Never has a visit to my doctor been so life-changing! Sure, I've grown to expect doctors' visits to be probing and personal…maybe even painful. But for me, this visit went well beyond all of that. Here, Dr. Gerhart dialogues with his patient in order to prescribe a cure that LASTS. Read on as this experienced physician reintroduces his patient to *the Great Physician…the One who brings true healing.*

—RICK CONRAD, PASTOR
INAUGURAL CHAIR, CHILDREN'S FELLOWSHIP OF INDIA
POSTGRADUATE RESEARCH IN SYSTEMATIC THEOLOGY,
UNIVERSITY OF ABERDEEN, SCOTLAND

Dr. Clark Gerhart's groundbreaking book provides an extraordinary insight into how the body and brain God gave us interact in our decision-making process—and especially the role played by the subconscious. This insight helps us recognize temptation earlier and deal with persistent sin in our life as we access the power of the Holy Spirit through prayer focused on the areas of temptation and sin. At the same time, it removes guilt from the natural functioning of brain and body that we may misunderstand as temptation or even sin. While helpful for every Christian, this book will be of special help to counselors and pastors not well-versed in medical aspects of brain and body functions.

—LES STOBBE
EDITOR IN CHIEF, JERRY B. JENKINS CHRISTIAN WRITERS' GUILD

Say Goodbye to Stubborn SIN

CLARK GERHART, MD
with Jefferson Scott

SAY GOODBYE TO STUBBORN SIN by Clark Gerhart, MD, with Jefferson Scott

This book or parts thereof may not be reproduced in any form, stored in a retrieval system, or transmitted in any form by any means—electronic, mechanical, photocopy, recording, or otherwise—without prior written permission of the publisher, except as provided by United States of America copyright law.

Unless otherwise noted, all Scripture quotations are from the New American Standard Bible, updated edition. Copyright © 1960, 1962, 1963, 1968, 1971, 1972, 1973, 1975, 1977, 1995 by the Lockman Foundation. Used by permission. (www.Lockman.org)

Scripture quotations marked ASV are from the American Standard Bible. Copyright © 1960, 1962, 1968, 1971, 1972, 1973, 1975, by the Lockman Foundation. Used by permission.

Scripture quotations marked KJV are from the King James Version of the Bible.

Scripture quotations marked NCV are from The Holy Bible, New Century Version. Copyright © 1987, 1988, 1991 by Word Publishing, Dallas, Texas 75039. Used by permission.

Scripture quotations marked NIV are from the Holy Bible, New International Version. Copyright © 1973, 1978, 1984, International Bible Society. Used by permission.

Scripture quotations marked TLB are from The Living Bible. Copyright © 1971. Used by permission of Tyndale House Publishers, Inc., Wheaton, IL 60189. All rights reserved.

Cover design by Rachel Campbell

Copyright © 2005 by Clark Gerhart, MD
All rights reserved

Library of Congress Cataloging-in-Publication Data
Gerhart, Clark.
　Say goodbye to stubborn sin / Clark Gerhart with Jefferson Scott.
　　p. cm.
　Includes bibliographical references.
　ISBN 9781711381664

Names, places, and identifying details with regard to stories in this book have been changed to protect the privacy of individuals who may have had similar experiences. The people referenced consist of composites of a number of people with similar issues, and the names and circumstances have been changed to protect their confidentiality. Any similarity between the names and stories of individuals described in this book to individuals known to readers is purely coincidental.

Printed in the United States of America

To my wife, Kim:

*Whose dedication to me has been proven
through time and many struggles.*

*Whose heart accepts so easily
the things I struggle with most.*

*Who has helped me to better understand what it means
to be God's bride simply by observing her.*

ACKNOWLEDGMENTS

Clark Gerhart

Special thanks goes out to my coauthor, Jefferson Scott, without whom this book would still be hidden away in my computer. His skill as a writer brought life to this manuscript, and his instruction and encouragement helped bring this medical writer into the Christian arena.

A great big thanks goes out to Strang Communications for supporting this project and not making me hear "We love the book, but..." one more time.

I also want to thank Pastor Rick Conrad, who reviewed my ideas and helped me to identify theological land mines. Even though he could not prevent me from stepping in all of them, he at least allowed me to know when to expect an explosion.

Just as helpful was the input of neuropharmacologist Tom Parry, PhD, who reviewed the manuscript and helped me keep my neurologic pathways straight.

I must also thank Marita and Florence Littauer for their inspiration during CLASSeminar, which helped moved me another step along the path toward becoming a Christian speaker and author, and for their contribution to the personality section in chapter 9.

This work could never have been accomplished without my wife, Kimberly, who lived this book with me during both the learning and the writing phases. Her steadfast love, along with the love and support of my great kids—Lindsay, Brendan, Brooke, and Chelsea—helped me through the ups and downs during the many years it took to bring this to print.

Finally, and most importantly, I have to thank the Lord for something I never would have thought I would thank Him for before this project began—struggling. The struggles He carefully designed for me allowed my flesh to be subdued and transformed into something pleasing to Him and something I hope will benefit you, the reader.

Jefferson Scott

I encountered the teachings of this book back in 2001. Clark graciously led me through the LASTS pathway way back then, and God used it to deliver me from a stronghold I thought I'd never be free of. When I had the opportunity to partner with Clark to bring this teaching to a wider audience, I jumped at it.

Thanks go to Clark for his openness to learning God's teachings we've tried to communicate in this book. Thanks for all the iron-sharpening-iron sessions, Clark, and for all the help on other projects. I'm still holding you to your promise to one day perform a surgery of my choice.

Thanks to the team at Strang Communications: Stephen Strang, who caught the vision for the book right away; Bert Ghezzi, who made it happen; Rachel Campbell, for her awesome cover; Barbara Dycus, for her excellent editorial feedback; Deborah Moss, for leaving in the contractions [grin]; and the rest of the team.

Thanks as always to my wife, Robin, for her steadfast love, to my children for being wonderful, and to my Lord for giving me the blessing of communicating His Word to the world.

A little science estranges men from God; much science leads them back to Him.

—Louis Pasteur

CONTENTS

Introduction — 1

Section 1
The Disease

1 The Symptoms — 9
2 The Illness — 23

Section 2
The Treatment

3 The Treatment Plan — 37
4 Homeostasis—Defending Your Steady State — 65
5 Drives—Fleshly Drivenness — 77
6 Reflexes—Conditioned Responses — 89
7 Senses—Living Just to Stimulate Your Receptors — 103
8 Subconscious Brain Functions—Programmed to Be Me — 121
9 Emotions—the Chemistry Behind Your Feelings — 139
10 Internal Rewards—Your Neurologic Motives — 155
11 Conscious Thought—Rational Thinking and the Will — 169

Section 3
The Cure

12 The Final Healing — 187
Conclusion — 203

INTRODUCTION

If I am a Christian, why do I keep struggling with this sin?

Why can't I get victory over this stupid thing for more than a few days at a time? It's like it owns me. I've tried everything—read the books, prayed the prayers, gone to the seminars—but I always end up right back here in the same place, hanging my head in guilt and defeat and leaning on God's forgiveness one more time. Will I ever beat this problem, or am I cursed to fight a losing battle with it until heaven?

Know what I mean? Have you ever been so frustrated with a problem that keeps coming around and around that you were almost ready to throw in the towel?

It may be those words that just fly out of your mouth whenever you're with a certain person. Or maybe it's where your mind—and your eyes—go whenever you're around someone of the opposite sex. Maybe it's what happens to you when that car keeps breaking down or that in-law keeps pushing your buttons. Maybe you've been trying to kick a habit, or you're facing an attitude you just can't change. Whatever it is, it has left you staggering. Is that where you are right now?

I've been there. Oh, yes, I know the place well.

For me it was an unrelenting case of unforgiveness. Sound lame? Sound easy to fix compared to addiction to cocaine or fits of spousal abuse? Well, maybe it is, but I can tell you that it was almost the end of me. The seething bitterness I felt had my marriage and closest relationships strained to the breaking point. My career was in jeopardy. My spiritual life was hanging by a thread. It had me in a death grip.

But now I can honestly tell you God has given me victory over that stubborn sin. I am free from it, praise God!

How did I get to that place of freedom? How did I finally gain victory over this chronic besetting sin? It started when I began to understand what my sinful, human nature was really all about. My medical training intersected with my spiritual journey, finally leading to the dramatic revelation that "the flesh," that not-quite-understood force inside us that doesn't want to obey God, truly is rooted in our *flesh*.

That may seem like a small thing, an obvious truth, but it really becomes a dramatic experience in your life when you realize that you can actually let your body teach you about your fleshly nature. Suddenly the flesh is not some vague mystical thing. It is as real as the nose on your face—in fact, it *is* the nose on your face. As you learn how your sense of smell and all of the other bodily functions work, it gives you a graphic demonstration of your fleshly nature in action and helps you understand why it is so powerful in your life.

This new understanding allowed me to spot areas of fleshly bondage in my life and to identify the underlying causes of my chronic struggles. Then I learned how to apply the power of God's grace directly to the source of my sin through confession, submission, and trust in His power. And victory was mine.

I've gotten there. So have many others who have encountered the teachings in this book. You can get to this place, too. You can have permanent victory over that area of sin that is eating you up inside.

Is anger your chronic struggle? Armed with the things you'll learn in these pages, you will be able to enter the same situation that normally sent you out of control and instead face it with perfect calm. Is bitterness the thing that keeps you in defeat? You can release your bitterness by the power of God—and find yourself released in the process. Is the rush of gambling the thing you just can't seem to beat? You can be free of its allure and its bitter sting. Is pornography what has you in its stranglehold? Through the teachings God has revealed to me, you can come to the place where you feel yourself actually desiring purity over that chemical rush.

INTRODUCTION

What is your archenemy that always manages to overtake you and leave you in misery? The one that leaves you crying out like Paul, "Wretched man that I am! Who will set me free from the body of this death?" (Romans 7:24). Whatever it is, if you're willing to expose yourself to God's power in the ways I show you, you will be giving Paul's cry of victory also: "Thank God! It has been done by Jesus Christ our Lord. He has set me free" (Romans 7:25, TLB).

Take Another Lap Through the Wilderness

Would you believe me if I told you that this struggle you're having is a sign of God's grace? Can you even imagine a world in which this cycle of temptation/resistance/giving in/self-loathing/confession/temptation is a good thing?

Well, it is.

Think about it: if you weren't God's child, you wouldn't be having this struggle. Without Christ, there is no real reason *not* to give in to every fleshly impulse and live it up, no matter whom it hurts. But you *are* struggling. You do hate this persistent problem. And that by itself is evidence that you have the Holy Spirit inside you telling you that what you're doing is wrong. So the struggle itself is a sign that God is working in your life.

He simply loves you too much to allow you to slink away into total corruption. But He also won't let you go on to the deeper things of God while you're still in your sin. He won't leave you like you are, but you can't go on, either. So, you're stuck.

It's not just you. God's people have been doing this since the children of Israel left Egypt. Their recurring sin was a lack of trust in God. You'd think they would've learned to trust Him when the Red Sea split open in front of them, but they didn't. So God sent them off for a little time in the wilderness to help in the learning process.

After a while they ran out of water. Did they trust God? No.

Back to the wilderness.

Next crisis: no food. Were they ready to trust Him yet? Nope.

One more lap in the wilderness.

At the edge of the Promised Land, God urged them to go in and take the place by faith, trusting in His power to drive out their enemies before them. It was time to trust again. Did they do it? Still no.

Back to the wilderness. Around and around they went, doing laps in the wilderness for forty years.

Is that how you feel? Like you are just going around in circles through a dry and desolate place in your life? Well, you can find victory. God never gave up on Israel. And He won't give up on you.

Just remember that the pain you experience in these difficult times is a sign of God's unending love for you. If He didn't want you fixed, He wouldn't devote so much time and effort to intervene in your life, to bring you back to His path. The key is submitting to the work God wants to do in you, and in the pages to come I'll show you just what is involved in that process.

"Doc, It Hurts When I Do This..."

I'm a surgeon. I make my living by causing people pain—but they keep coming to me! And, of course, you know why: the pain I cause is pain that will lead to healing.

So it is with God. The material I cover in this book is designed to help you in the healing process—but it may cause you pain, too. The path to health is not always easy. The more ingrained the sin, the more pain it may cause as the Great Physician works to remove it. But just as no patient has ever asked me to put his tumor back in, so you will never regret the discomfort when God cuts into your flesh. In His hands is true healing.

I've decided to present this book following a very familiar structure for me and possibly for you: a visit to the doctor.

Most people, when they first go to the doctor, have no idea what's happening inside. All they know is that it hurts. So the first thing we're going to do, in Section 1, "The Disease," is sit and discuss your symptoms and talk about the disease process that is making you ill. In that section I'll teach you a little about how problems arise from the flesh and try to give you a better understanding of where the pain is coming from—and why it's so important that you get treated.

Then we'll head to my office, where I'll explain to you how we're going to approach this disease. Section 2, "The Treatment," details an aggressive, fivefold plan of attack called LASTS: listening, admitting, submitting, trusting, and standing firm. Here you'll come to understand how to bring every area of fleshly control back under the authority of Jesus Christ.

Also in this section we'll take your body's systems one by one. It'll be up on the examination table for you. We'll see how amazing your body is, and how sin has usurped some of those systems, impelling you to sin.

You might think you have an idea what the flesh is like, but once you see how your natural physiology helps to produce your fleshly nature, your flesh will be clearly visible in your life. You won't be wearing one of those drafty gowns, but as God reveals your hidden sins, you may feel just as exposed.

You'll learn about how your neurologic pathways and the brain's internal reward system, as well as many other processes, make you do the things you do. Before too many pages you might feel you've enrolled in med school. But don't worry; I promise to make it understandable and easy to use in everyday life. It's at this point that you may find yourself saying, "Aha, that explains why I do that!" Many people have found this section to be full of life-changing revelations.

Finally we'll look at "The Cure," the final healing that only God can bring. This is where we'll get an x-ray of a flesh that is being slowly but surely sanctified by the work of the Holy Spirit.

THE PICTURE OF HEALTH

Right now, as you begin the process of dealing with your flesh, you might think that simply ending the recurring struggle in your life would be enough. I mean, what could be better than finally throwing off this sin, this horrible weight that's been holding you down for so long?

But there's more. If you commit yourself fully to this process, you will know far better benefits than this. After God walks you through this important stage of your Christian life, your spiritual world will change. You will think differently and act differently. You may find that some of what you said you believed in the past was only lip service. Now it will be real.

As you stick with this process, your spiritual strength will grow. Indeed, you will experience some of the greatest power in life—the power to change a human life. Your life, certainly, but not yours only. People around you will be touched as the change that God has done in you bubbles over.

As you stay with this sanctification process (because that's what we're really talking about here: God's work of sanctification), you will develop the type of closeness with God you've always craved, that world-class walk with Christ. It's a closeness that soldiers sharing a foxhole feel in wartime. You will come to understand that He will never leave you or forsake you. You will not be perfect, of course, but you will have confidence knowing that your imperfections will never separate you from the love of God. When you truly understand how the flesh works, it will be as if scales fall from your eyes. The world, people around you, current events, major crimes, and even stories from the Bible itself will suddenly snap into sharp focus. *Oh!* you'll say, *now I understand why that happened. I can't believe I've never been able to see this before!*

In the end, the anguish you're feeling now over this recurring sin will be replaced with a quiet assurance and inner joy that comes from facing the worst in yourself and surviving. You'll know the joy of being finally liberated from a wicked thing that has had you in a stranglehold for years. Once you have stood with God through tough times, you will know that He is beside you and nothing can shake you.

At times you may feel like the sanctification process is full of struggles, but you will find that God's goal in this cleansing process is to prepare you to receive His greatest blessings. So take heart! There are blessings piled atop blessings waiting for you at the end of this difficult journey.

Are you ready?

If so, the doctor will see you now.

SECTION 1

THE DISEASE

CHAPTER 1

THE SYMPTOMS

BECKY

When a dent begins forming in Becky's forehead she finally lifts her head off the steering wheel where it's been resting. After driving around aimlessly for hours, she's finally found herself in a corner of Community Park, slumped over the steering wheel, crying.

The engagement is off. What a disaster. As soon as she'd left the man she thought she'd spend the rest of her life with, she had run to her mother's house, hoping for consolation. But her mother hadn't been home. Why? Because she'd been over at Rick's place. Rick, Becky's spoiled brother. It's too much. Too much that her mother isn't there for her in her time of need. And way too much that it was *him* who has taken her away when she needs her more.

Becky stares out the window at the children playing with their mothers. Her heart aches to see the joy on their faces. How many times has she wished she could feel what those kids are feeling right now? Why can't she ever have that? A bitter rage grows in her chest. Her parents have done this to her. Especially Mom. It hurts so much she begins to tremble and even starts to feel nauseated. She feels trapped inside her car, glassed off from life.

Part of her wants to drive to her brother's and unleash her rage at both of them right now. See how *they* like the pain for a change. Another part of her wants to drive straight into the lake and be done with it all.

She's not conscious of this other feeling going on inside her, but somehow, in some strange way, this familiar resentment feels good.

Her mind flashes back over dozens of memories of her parents preferring her younger brother over her. She can remember every slight, every unequal treatment. She can remember all the way back to when Rick got twenty-five dollars to spend on his tenth birthday, though she had only received ten dollars at hers.

It feels stupid to be so worked up over something that happened that long ago. But it burns like acid in her heart. Tears well up in her eyes all over again. But she's all grown up now. She's beyond all that adolescent garbage. Now she knows how to be content in Christ with or without the approval of her parents.

Where, then, after all these years, has this turmoil come from?

Todd

Todd has a problem with pornography. Internet porn, magazines, movies—even commercials on TV and his wife's clothes catalogs cause him to stumble.

For a while he kept it hidden. Magazines only when traveling alone. Movies only in hotel rooms. The Internet only when no one else is home or awake. He's gotten very good at hiding his dirty little secret. But inside, he's in agony. He's been a Christian for twenty years. He's a Sunday school teacher, for crying out loud. What is he doing ogling these images?

He's desperate to get out of this pit. He pleads for God to deliver him. He's read books, visited addiction support Web pages, downloaded twelve-step Bible studies. He even has a couple of accountability partners he goes to lunch with once a week. But the problem remains. Lately things have gotten worse. He can't worship at church anymore because one of the women on the worship team turns him on. Women and teenage girls in the pews around him make him nervous. He's scared of himself, of what he might do given half a chance.

Worse, his wife's onto him now. She was searching for something on the Internet and saw in the history folder some of the places he'd been to. She asked him point-blank to explain himself. He confessed everything. She was mad and compassionate at the same time. She's forgiven him, but she hasn't forgotten. Now the game has shifted. Now it's all about keeping it secret from her. Their relationship is in crisis on all fronts now.

He feels awful. Wretched. What kind of a monster is he? He wonders where God is in all of it. Worse, he feels helpless against this overpowering urge to feast his eyes on lust-invoking images.

And in a part of his heart he would never tell anyone about, he's not completely sure he wants to let go of the lust. It makes him feel so good, after all, so excited and alive and lost in ecstasy—at least for a while. What could the boring old "righteous life" offer that feels anything near as good as this?

Going Deep

Anything about Becky or Todd sound familiar? Maybe the stubborn sin you battle isn't unforgiveness or pornography, but I imagine there are points of similarity between your issue and theirs. We're going to discover that their real "disease" isn't what they thought it was. The surface sin, the behavior they couldn't manage to curb, is what they're focused on. It's the sin they see and agonize over. But we're going to see that the top-level sin isn't really the problem. There's something deeper.

Get ready to make the same discovery about your chronic struggle, too. You may think it's about the anger or the overspending or the addiction. But in reality there's something beneath it all causing the problem. That "something else" is like radioactive waste on the ocean floor. It sits down there endlessly generating all sorts of mutated creatures that wash up on the beach (the surface sins). If you like, you can spend all your time sweeping the shoreline and carrying away the foul things that surface. But if you really want to fix the problem once and for all, you have to go deep.

But we'll begin at the top. The surface sins point us to the general area where the waste is hidden below. To shift metaphors, we'll begin our search for the root problem the way a doctor begins his quest for a patient's true problem: by listening to the symptoms.

As a doctor listening to a patient describing his symptoms, I usually begin to get a hunch about what might be going on inside him. That's when I start asking probing questions. Because you've picked up this book, that probably means you're a Christian struggling with a chronic sin. Galatians 5:19–21 tells us that sin of all sorts occurs because of the flesh, so already I have one of these hunches: I have a hunch that your problem has something to do with an area of your flesh that is not under God's control.

In this chapter we will look at the common symptoms people notice when their flesh, not God, is controlling their life. Consider them my probing questions. See if one or more of them describes what you're feeling.

```
Lack of self-control
```
The most obvious sign that the flesh is in control of a Christian is when you do the thing you swore you'd never do again. You feel this urgency pressing on you. Then something seems to take control, and you suddenly find yourself doing or saying something you'd hoped was forever in your past.

You're laying out the credit card again, or you're lashing out at the kids again, or you're polishing off every dessert in the house again, or you're prowling the Internet porn sites again. Or maybe you find yourself violating your own boundaries—doing awful things that disgust yourself—and wondering how you ever got to this point.

"I can't help myself!" a part of you cries. "I was going along just fine, and then wham! Somehow I was neck-deep in that behavior again! How can I say I'm walking with Christ when I go back to this awful thing over and over?"

Your feelings of helplessness are a sure sign that your flesh, not God's Spirit, is ruling you in this area. In those moments you really are not in control. You truly are under the command of your flesh.

If there's one thing I want you to get from this book, it's this: at whatever point your flesh is ruling you, you are sinning. Because if you're a Christian, you'll serve either the flesh or God's Spirit. There are no other choices. (If you're not a Christian, you'll have no other choice but to serve the flesh.) Where the Spirit of the Lord is, there is freedom (2 Corinthians 3:17), but where the control of the flesh is, there is only bondage (Romans 6:16).

I want you to take your flesh seriously. If it is ruling you at any point, it is the thing that is holding you back from the kind of walk with Christ you've always longed to have.

But if you find yourself in this situation, I don't want you to be discouraged. You've found this book, and in this book I will tell you how to bring this very area of helplessness—this part of your life in which you are truly out of control—into the pure light of God's sanctifying Spirit. You may be out of control now, but it doesn't have to be that way. The fruit of the Spirit is self-control.

Wretchedness

The single most common complaint given by people struggling with their flesh is a feeling of wretchedness. People with stubborn sins often complain of feeling deeply ashamed of their repeated sin—ashamed, dirty, horrified, and embarrassed. They may feel worthless. They hate the sin they commit, and yet they keep committing it. In short, they feel wretched.

If this is happening to you, it's actually a good thing. You see, if you're wretched over a repeated sin, it's because there is something good in you—Christ's righteousness and a redeemed spirit—that objects to sin. No, it loathes sin. So when you commit this habitual sin, part of you loathes what you yourself are doing.

In Romans 14:22, Paul says we're happiest when we don't condemn ourselves for our choices. Or, turning the idea around, we can say that we're most miserable when we do condemn ourselves for the choices we make. One half of you despises the other, and the two sides are tearing you apart. That, my friend, is wretchedness.

Wretched Christians sometimes begin to believe they are too awful for even God to love. They wonder if God has put a cap on His love because they've reached their seventy-times-seven forgiveness limit. After all, who could continue to forgive such a hardened sinner after so many despicable transgressions?

Are your confessions sounding empty even to you? Have failure and defeat replaced the joy and victory you thought the Christian life was supposed to bring? If so, I imagine you're crying out with Paul: "Wretched man that I am! Who will set me free from the body of this death?" (Romans 7:24). This wretchedness is a clue that the flesh is active in your life.

`Turmoil`

One of the most characteristic symptoms of a problem with the flesh is a sense of inner turmoil. Are you carrying a deep sense of unresolved anxiety that feels like you are wrestling with an inner force? The problem is that you really are wrestling with an inner force—two, actually. This constant turmoil comes from the fact that your flesh and spirit are battling back and forth over the area of recurring sin.

Sometimes this turmoil is mild. It's this nagging anxiety always stirring at the back of your mind. Sometimes it's much worse, coming even to the point of captivating your every thought by day and stealing away your rest at night.

The reason for this turmoil is that you're holding to two opposing opinions about this recurring sin at the same time. On the one hand, you hate it. On the other, you love it. Psychologists call this *cognitive dissonance*, and it is a miserable state to find yourself in.

I once owned a car that kept breaking down. No matter how much I paid or how long it spent in the shop, it would always break down again. And again. It was driving me insane. My friends said, "What's the big deal? Just fix it." But for me it *was* a big deal. Deep inside it was tearing me apart. I lost sleep over it, wondering why this was happening to me. During the day while I went about my obligations, I was constantly wrestling with what I should do about it. The car problem was just a car problem, after all. But the inner turmoil was a severe struggle—a sign of something deeper going on.

Eventually, I recognized the turmoil as a symptom of God wanting to do a work of cleansing in my flesh, and I responded to Him on the car issue. In the end God dealt with attitudes of materialism, professionalism, and pride, and *voilà!* The car problems disappeared.

A woman I know experienced a time of struggling while trying to adopt a child. Concern over the issue seemed to distract her much more than seemed appropriate. To me, with my four children, it didn't seem like such a big deal. But for her it was all consuming. Through the experience she realized that God wanted to address something else deep down. As she struggled, she grew in faith and trust in God in the process. Not long after, the adoption problems ceased. She now has a beautiful little girl as a trophy of her victory over her flesh.

Are you fixated on something right now? Is there something captivating your mind, distracting you during the day and leaving you sleepless at night? If so, recognize it as a symptom of something deeper that needs to be addressed.

Exaggeration

Another classic sign that there's trouble down deep is that you tend to blow things out of proportion. Problems seem exaggerated. You get overly upset over what others consider trivial matters.

Has this ever happened to you? Have you been like someone I know who was upset about something in his marriage but ended up tearing the paper towel dispenser off the public restroom wall because it wouldn't work right? His frustration over the real problem was simmering just under the surface, needing only a slight provocation to send him over the top. His outer anger was a sign of an inner problem.

It's not only anger. You may cry uncontrollably over a minor frustration or become almost suicidal after a trivial setback. Do you feel wracked with guilt over a small infraction? Are you vacillating helplessly over decisions you once made with ease? Have you ever felt like quitting your job and leaving the state because of a problem with a person at work? Do you find yourself blurting out responses that leave everyone around you asking, "Where did that remark come from?"

If so, it may be because there is another problem deep inside you that is adding energy to your responses to superficial issues. Recognize this as a tip-off that somewhere underneath it all something else is wrong.

Confusion

A common symptom of a problem with the flesh is confusion. Your whole life seems to have been thrown into confusion, and everything's suddenly too complex.

Perhaps you've always thought you had your life pretty well planned out, but suddenly your plans are falling through left and right. For years you thought you'd found your life's mate, but now you're not so sure. Your job used to be challenging and fulfilling, but now you're wondering if you're in the wrong business altogether. Decisions as straightforward as selecting a piece of furniture or buying a car become complex when you are wrestling inside with priorities, goals, and principles.

The most disturbing part of confusion is when it is confusion toward God. "Why is this happening to me, God? If Your Word is true, why do I keep failing? Why am I not experiencing the love, joy, and peace other Christians seem to have? Are You even hearing my prayers?" You may begin to doubt your salvation, the truth of the Bible—even the very existence of God.

If this is you, don't worry: it's normal to be confused in your situation. After all, no one ever walked up to the pulpit and said, "If you give your life to Christ, you will have misery, turmoil, and despair!" They promised inner peace and a quiet kind of joy that the world will find baffling. So when you're not experiencing it, it's natural to be scratching your head.

But don't get mad at the preachers. What they said is true. That *is* what the victorious Christian life is like when the flesh is in check. Unfortunately, we tend to spend most of our time talking about the victory we *should* have and very little time dealing with the flesh in real terms so we can actually attain that victory. So that's what we intend to do here. Once you have broken through to victory in this area of your life, you'll be ready to enjoy the blessings they described.

Hang on to that picture of the Christian life. It's a vision of where you're headed. At present your flesh is ruling you at one or more points. That's why you're feeling defeated and confused. But when that area is brought under the control of Jesus Christ, you will finally get to enter that promised land.

Repetition

An obvious symptom of an unresolved fleshly issue is when a particular problem seems to return over and over. We don't call something *stubborn sin* if it happened only once. The Bible doesn't

The Symptoms

pull any punches with its description: "Like a dog that returns to its vomit is a fool who repeats his folly" (Proverbs 26:11). *Ew.* That's what it feels like, isn't it? You feel like you've been back to this same mess countless times, like you're somehow connected to it. You feel like it's a part of you, and therefore you can never gain victory over it. "That's just how I am, I guess."

Look for recurring patterns in your life. Do you always seem to have run-ins with authority figures? Do you always overeat when you're under pressure? When you're out with certain friends, do you always end up making the same mistakes?

Let's say you had a problem with a teacher in high school who hassled you over your behavior. You finally graduate and think you're leaving the problem teacher behind. But what do you find at college? A professor just like him. You drop his class, finish school, thinking you're leaving the problem behind you. But guess what you find in the form of your first boss? Leave the job, and you will struggle with leadership at church. Leave the church, and you will find yourself struggling with a policeman upset that you violated the speed limit.

At some point you may want to consider the possibility that maybe the world isn't actually filled with people who cause you problems. It could be that you keep getting into the same situation over and over because the problem is with you.

Are there any recurring complaints you run into all the time? Any negative comments people seem to always make about you? Look for patterns. They are symptoms of a deeper problem. In a way, they are markers leading you to the root issue. In a future chapter I'll show you how to follow those markers.

As I was writing this book, I had an experience that illustrates this beautifully. I received an e-mail from a friend who, because of a lack of messages from me, felt that I was upset with him and was expressing my displeasure by withholding communication. He admitted he tended to be a people-pleaser, and he knew that he might be reading too much into my lack of response, but he was upset nonetheless. I wrote back and told him he was wrong and that he had read too much into my lack of messages.

A funny (or not so funny) thing happened the very next day, however. My wife, who also tends to be a bit of a people-pleaser, got upset with me over a disagreement we had had recently. She said I always withheld affection and communication from her whenever I wanted to express my displeasure. This made her feel like she had to please me in some way, and it was causing her stress. I heard myself answering her with the same words I'd used with my friend: "You're just too much of a people-pleaser, honey. You read too much into my silence. You're wrong."

Suddenly my own words dawned on me: "Look for patterns—similar types of people, similar situations, similar accusations." I had to stop and think: could it be that the recent problems were a symptom of God at work deep inside trying to get me to deal with an issue? Of course, it was. So I apologized to my friend and my wife—and now know that this is an area of my flesh that God wants brought under His control.

Learn to recognize repetitive characteristics in your problems to see when the underlying battle with the flesh is causing you to struggle.

Despair

A sure sign that you're struggling with the flesh is despair, a hopelessness that you will never gain victory over this problem.

If you're a Christian, you have access to more power than you could contain. So why hasn't that power been able to get rid of this problem in your life? Maybe you're like the guy whose rowboat has a hole in it. You're bailing frantically, so why are you still sinking? Because you haven't addressed the real problem. You have to get down to the bottom of the boat and fix the hole.

How many years have you been bailing? Because you've picked up this book, I'm guessing you've been battling like this for a long time. You're beyond frustration now. You're beyond discouragement. How many years of failure and misery does it take to beat a person down, anyway? Maybe you're beginning to think you're just unfixable. Better to resign yourself to defeat and try to minimize the damage.

That's despair talking. And despair is a symptom of a deeper illness that needs to be targeted for healing.

The Symptoms

Stagnation

Feel like you're getting nowhere with this problem? Feel like you're taking a hundred laps around Mount Sinai? Feel drier than a cardboard box in the Sahara? It's a common sign that your flesh is ruling you in a certain area of your life. You're probably feeling it most in your spiritual life. Your prayers go unanswered. Your quiet times are boring. The Bible seems closed to you. You're finding worship dull and repetitive. And you don't really feel like going to the church fellowship, thank you very much.

Possibly your life seems to lack direction right now, too. Has it been a long time since you had any specific guidance from God? Do you feel like dropping out of every ministry activity you're involved in? How could you go out and tell people about the joys of the Christian life, anyway? This stagnation is a sign that your flesh is quenching the Spirit in your life.

But be encouraged: this is something that can be fixed. But don't miss this as a symptom of a deep problem.

Oppression

Another common symptom you may be experiencing over this stubborn sin is a feeling of oppression. It is as if you have a boulder on your back that is slowly crushing you into the earth. It causes you to feel weak, emotionally and even physically. It weighs on your countenance, pulling it down also. Everything is too heavy and too hard. It may look very much like clinical depression—in fact, it may actually *be* clinical depression. But the cause of this depression is not a medical malady.

The oppression you feel is very likely the result of God reaching down and placing His finger on the area of your flesh He wants addressed. And once He points it out, He presses on you—softly at first, but then progressively harder—until you can feel deep inside that there is a problem.

Once again, this is good news of a sort. God is putting this pressure on you because He longs for you to give up the sin that is at the root of your habitual failures. He wants you free of this entangling sin so you can go on to maturity and fullness in Him. This is His fatherly urging, leading you to sanctification. If you learn to recognize this symptom as a message from God, it can lead you directly to the area of flesh that's causing you so much misery.

Conflict

Are you fighting with everybody these days? Are you butting heads with your spouse, your boss, your friends, even your children? If so, there's a possibility that it might not actually be everyone else who's having the bad day. It may be an indicator that your flesh is out of God's control.

These conflicts shouldn't be so surprising. You're at war with yourself—of course it's going to spread to those around you.

My oldest son learned this one firsthand. His younger brother had gotten a new pet, a baby iguana, so the older boy decided he would set up a heat lamp for the little lizard. After only half-listening to the instructions, he set it on the cage, turned it on, and walked away. The heat lamp quickly melted the plastic lid, filling the cage with fumes and killing the iguana.

You can imagine the conflict that followed when his brother found out.

My wife and I knew what the problem was. We had been trying to get him to grow in responsibility for some time. Now conflict arose to "help" him recognize the problem. Unfortunately, the iguana became a casualty in my son's battle with the flesh.

In the same way, it is likely that casualties are mounting around you as your battle progresses. If your flesh is controlling you to the point that conflict is spilling out onto those around you, it is usually the ones you love most who will suffer for your problem. Those closest to you will become collateral damage as they come into contact with the battle going on inside of you.

When your flesh is out of God's control, that's bad. But the worst of it is when your out-of-control flesh strikes someone else's out-of-control flesh. The result is a "flesh fest," where two (or more!) people hurl their fleshly responses back and forth without restraint. This can destroy a relationship.

If you find yourself in constant conflict with others, take it as a clue that your flesh is calling the shots in your life. Even if somebody else started it, nothing would've started at all if your flesh hadn't arisen to the insult.

Review Your Symptoms

Well, how are you feeling now? I've asked some probing questions about your flesh. Did I nail it on one or two of them? On all of them, maybe?

If so, I would have to conclude that the reason you can't gain lasting victory over this stubborn, habitual sin is that in some area of your life *the flesh is in charge.* It is at work trying to direct you and rule you.

We don't know where that area is yet. That will take a much more thorough examination. But at least we know what we're dealing with now. Our goal is to find this area of your flesh and bring it back under God's control. That is the sole purpose of this book.

In the next chapter we'll continue our first visit as patient and doctor. We'll move from discussing your symptoms to where I will explain the nature of the disease and lay out our strategy for tackling it.

CHAPTER 2

THE ILLNESS

ALL right, so you've explained your symptoms and I've asked you a few questions that may have come a bit too close to the mark for comfort. We've been through the first phase of the doctor's visit, and now I'm inviting you back to my office for a consultation. After some preliminaries, I'm going to explain the nature of what I suspect is behind your symptoms, and I'm going to lay out a strategy for going forward toward healing.

What It Isn't

As I listen to a patient's answers to my probing questions, I begin to form a *differential diagnosis*. This is simply a list of all the things that *could* be behind the symptoms the patient is describing. My task is to then go down this list, eliminating the ones that aren't causing the problem until we arrive at the one that is.

That's what we'll be doing here. We'll go through the list of things that might be causing your chronic problems to see if we can rule out the ones that are unlikely. This will leave us with the most likely underlying cause of your problems, which we will use as our *working diagnosis*. The working diagnosis will then help direct our next series of tests, which will eventually lead us to a *final diagnosis* and a cure.

All right, let's go down the list of things you might think *could* be causing your problem (but probably aren't).

Satan

The devil made me do it!

Wouldn't it be nice if we could blame all our sins on Satan, like Flip Wilson's character Geraldine used to do on the old *Flip Wilson Show*? That way we could go on sinning (and enjoying the short-term benefits of sin) without having to take responsibility for it or try to stop. But God doesn't give us that option. While it might be argued that non-Christians are heavily influenced by evil (2 Timothy 2:26), Christians are not. Christians have been set free from Satan's power and transferred from the domain of darkness into the kingdom of Christ (Colossians 1:13).

This isn't to say that Christians aren't assaulted by spiritual forces of evil. We certainly are! Neil T. Anderson, in his book *The Bondage Breaker*, estimates that 85 percent of Christians in America live under some type of influence from evil spiritual forces.[1] But we are not left unprotected. The Bible shows us in Job that God places a hedge around His children to protect us from Satan (Job 1:10). Before Satan could affect Job's life in the slightest, he had to come to God for permission.

The same is true for you. For Satan to affect your life, he must first go through God. And even then, God carefully monitors Satan's actions in the lives of His children. He allows Satan to intervene only as it fulfills God's own divine purposes for your sanctification and His glory.

One thing Satan can never do is force you to obey him. When you became a Christian, you were set free from Satan's ownership, and now you belong to Christ. All you have to do is resist Satan, and he will flee from you and the power of God within you (James 4:7). You can still choose to obey your old master and hang on to that pet sin, but the devil isn't making you do it. God has given you the keys to your chains, so if Satan continues to enslave you, it is something in you allowing him that control.

The world

The world we live in is certainly a possible cause of problems for us. We are immersed in the political, economic, and social systems that control the world around us and attempt to control our lives as well. The world surrounds us every day everywhere we go. By its sheer magnitude it has a profound affect on us.

What's more, nearly the entire world is designed to appeal to the flesh. Just watch a half-hour of prime-time television or walk through a mall, and it will easily prove my point. This world is designed to engage and enthrall our fleshly senses and desires. Lost people—and too many of us Christians—live to indulge our flesh and feast on the sensory rewards the world offers.

But for all that, we can't say the world *causes* us to sin, any more than we can say that Satan does. The world provides many opportunities to sin and many enticements to sin, even pressures to sin, but it can't force us to sin.

How has the world pressured you? Have you struggled at work because you wouldn't carry out some unethical demand your boss asked of you? Do you feel drawn, even dragged, toward lustful and sensual media? Have you faced pressure from neighbors because you said you wanted your kids to be home-schooled? Does the pressure to keep up with the Joneses keep you spending all your time working and away from family and church?

Being in this world is like sitting in an FBI interrogation. The harsh light is on you, and there are any number of forces screaming in your face to get you to cave in. At times you succumb to its enticements. At other times you remain strong.

Have you ever wondered why some temptations really get to you and others bounce off with no effect? I believe the ones that really make you sweat are those that seek to engage you at a point where your flesh is already controlling you.

Take me, for instance. I have had trouble dealing with the temptation to be resentful and unforgiving. It has caused a lot of struggling in my life. It's the problem that made me feel like Rocky Balboa facing Apollo Creed. That was me, trying to fight the problem but getting my face pounded over and over.

At the same time, the pressure to prioritize my career and cut a few corners in my Christian faith is also often present, but it has never been such a big deal to me. My professional life has even suffered at times because I should've been out on the golf course with influential colleagues on Sundays rather than in church. It was no great sacrifice; it just came naturally.

What's the difference? Why was I able to resist the one pressure but caved in to the other? In one area the flesh was still active, and in the other the flesh was under control. When you've given the Holy Spirit control, even the temptations that once did you in will just not look as good as they used to. That's when we begin to experience the spiritual victory Christ promised when He said that in this world we would have hardships but that He has overcome the world (John 16:33).

You say you're not quite the overcomer Christ promised? Your out-of-control flesh is giving in to the world's enticements? Well, I certainly understand, but you're not giving in to *every* temptation the world throws at you. The ones that succeeded in tripping you up did so because in those areas you were already off-balance. The world wouldn't have been able to cause you to stumble had you not had a problem in this area to begin with.

Worldly enticements do not cause the flesh to be out of control. The problem isn't with the world but with you and me and our flesh.

Other people

If I'm mad, it's your fault.

Have you heard yourself say something like that? What about these: "That woman is driving me to drink." "I wouldn't even be interested in that guy at the office if my husband would take a little time to pay attention to me." "If you wouldn't frustrate me, I wouldn't have to get so angry!"

Other people are the most visible, handy excuses for our own sin. It started when we were little—"Yes, I hit him, but only because he hit me first!"—and has continued right up until this moment.

No doubt there really are people around you who are in the wrong. Jerks, cheats, and crooks seem to dramatically outnumber the nice people (like you and me, of course). People are constantly cutting us off, cheating us out, or shouting us down. Their behavior triggers a desire in us to strike back.

But I'm afraid I have some bad news for you: if you sin in these situations, the problem is yours, not theirs. These other people may be doing things that appeal to your fleshly desires to respond in sin, but no one makes you go ahead and act on your temptation. No one but you. If you find you are continually baited in a certain way, that's another pointer that can help you locate the problem deep within your flesh. But I hope you can see which way it's pointing: at you, not them.

This doesn't mean that everyone else is innocent. Your wife may truly have a problem with communication. But if you respond by hitting her, the problem is yours. Your boss may really have wrongly promoted someone over you, but if your life is being torn apart by inner turmoil because of it, the problem is in you.

How is it that two people can face the same aggravation from another person and one of them act out in sin and the other pass the test just fine? Why did most people come out of the World War II concentration camps bitter and hateful while some, like Corrie ten Boom, emerged unconsumed by resentment? I know that even Corrie ten Boom felt the sting of resentment, but the difference was she wasn't controlled by it. Why? She had conquered the flesh in this area and was therefore able to give a Spirit-controlled response.

But isn't it possible to have the flesh under control and still be wronged by others? Yes, of course. And I believe that nothing is harder to bear than suffering wrongfully. Still, we have a great cloud of witnesses around us who have done just that, not least of whom is Jesus. If you are suffering for doing right, Jesus promises you real joy and the peace of a martyr (Matthew 5:11–12). The pain of the offense will be there, yes, but the symptoms of an inner battle that we have discussed will not.

In your interaction with other people, if you're experiencing the symptoms of a flesh that's in control, the problem is yours not theirs. You can't control other people anyway.

The Nature of the Illness

OK, we've worked through our differential diagnosis, crossing out the causes that we thought were possible but have been revealed not to be the causes of the problem. We've established that while other people, Satan, and the world around you can certainly trip you up, these are not where this recurring sin in your life comes from. I hope you're ready to admit that this is a problem in you, and that it is there—in you—where healing needs to happen. It's time for me to announce my final diagnosis.

Imagine we're in my office. I'm leaning back in my chair. My office is warm but professional. You see framed diplomas, weighty books on wooden shelves, and a light board for viewing X-rays. Now imagine me leaning forward thoughtfully. "Would you like to know what I think is going on inside you? Would you like to hear my theory about what is causing these symptoms to arise and what is behind the fact that you simply can't seem to get victory over this behavior, no matter what you try?"

My guess is that you would nod your head. "Yes, please tell me."

At that point I would go on to describe the basic physiology behind the illness you are suffering from. So let's do just that.

Understanding the problem in your flesh requires reviewing some basic facts about your salvation. Before you became a Christian, there was only one ruler in the Kingdom of You: the flesh. It's the me-first champion of the world. We see it in toddlers, and we see it in traffic. Our society revolves around the flesh, caters to it, is ruled by it, is battered by it, and seeks to satiate it. Before you came to Christ, you were part of the system in which flesh ruled all.

Then Jesus came into your heart. Your spirit was renewed, the Holy Spirit took up residence, and you became a new creation. You were brought from death to life, and you became a child of God.

That's good news for you, but bad news for the one who had been in power up to that point. What salvation meant to your flesh was that it was no longer *numero uno*. And if there's one thing your flesh doesn't like, it's being anything but Number One. The me-first champion of the world doesn't do second place very well. And so it does what any dethroned monarch would do: It starts a revolution. It exerts all of its power in a tireless campaign to reclaim its position of sovereignty in your life.

So there you are as a new Christian. The Bible tells us that the flesh and the Spirit are mortal enemies: "The flesh sets its desire against the Spirit, and the Spirit against the flesh; for these are in opposition to one another" (Galatians 5:17). And just as you can't put feuding siblings in a room together and expect things to go smoothly, so the flesh and the Spirit can't exist inside the same person without conflict.

If you are a Christian, you have undoubtedly felt the rumblings of this battle in your life, even though you may have never recognized the source until now. As the conflict rages inside, its effects eventually find their way to the surface. You'll be able to spot them easily—they're the symptoms we looked at in chapter one.

What Is the Flesh, Anyway?

But this all sounds like standard religious stuff, right? "Yeah, yeah, I know: I have to control my 'old fleshly nature'—the 'old man' I hear about from the pulpit. I have to crucify my flesh. Yada, yada, yada. I've heard it a thousand times and it's never helped, so why should it be any different now?"

My guess is that the reason it's never helped you, and the reason it doesn't help many people, is that you've never really understood what the flesh is. "Flesh," "sinful nature," "the old man"—what in the world do those mean, anyway? You're left with this vague, mystical notion of some disembodied force loose in your life. With such a nebulous picture of your enemy, no wonder you've been having trouble fighting it. Worse yet, if you're like most people, you've probably been trying to fight the flesh by simply exerting the power of the flesh—by "trying harder," a strategy that is doomed from the start.

The Bible, it turns out, is quite clear about what the flesh is. It's just that somehow we've missed it. The flesh, Paul says, is...the flesh.

Sounds like a trick answer, doesn't it? The sinful nature inside you, the old man that we are to take off, the flesh that is opposed to the Spirit, is actually embedded in your body and its systems. Bones, blood, muscles, neurons, hormones, nerves—your whole physical body—is where your human nature comes from. The flesh is rooted in your physiological body.

Paul refers to it by the Greek word *sarx*. This word means "the soft substance of the living body, which covers the bones and is permeated with blood," according to *Thayer's Greek Lexicon*.

The definition goes on to say that whenever the Bible uses *sarx* in contrast to *pneuma* (spirit), it "denotes mere human nature, the earthly nature of man apart from divine influence, and therefore prone to sin and opposed to God."[2]

There it is, as plain as can be. When Paul says *flesh* he means *flesh*, the human body and its natural functions, which is responsible for producing our human nature that is prone to sin. That's our enemy.

Tough to believe? Yeah, I know. That's because we are conditioned to believe that Paul used *sarx* figuratively, as if he were describing some metaphysical aspect of our being. But I believe God inspired Paul to describe *the body* as an essential component of our fleshly, sinful nature in order to help us learn what our flesh is really like.

If the body really is the flesh, in Paul's sense, then it gives us a new angle of attack in our spiritual war. We can take what we know about our bodies and use it to better understand how the flesh, the sinful nature, works in our lives—and how to defeat it.

That's what we're going to be doing for much of this book: looking at how our sinful nature is thoroughly rooted in our physical bodies. Once we can see how it's affecting us, we can see where we need to bring it under God's control. We're going to find out how completely fleshly we are as humans. And we're going to see how complex our physical beings are—which means that our sin nature is just as complex, which may explain why it is so difficult to deal with sometimes.

The most important idea to take away from this discussion is that the flesh is not some hazy, metaphysical force that we bring up occasionally in church and then forget about the rest of the week. In reality, the flesh is rooted in a mass of interconnecting processes that affect us 24/7, whether we understand them or not. It is who we are, through and through, from head to toe. And it is infected with a terrible illness called *sin*, from which it is desperately in need of healing.

Your body is sick. Not with the flu, perhaps, but certainly with sin. The good news is that now that we know where the problem is located, we can come up with a strategy for finding a cure. The goal of all medical treatment is to return the patient to health if possible.

If illness comes in and messes up the body's natural functions in an area, physicians intervene to try to restore everything back to working order. So it is with the flesh. Once it was good and healthy, but an illness (sin) has come in and messed things up. Our goal here is to return the flesh to goodness and health.

Not used to thinking of the flesh as good, are you? I can understand why. If preachers ever talk about the flesh at all, it's spoken of as a bad thing. And I haven't helped—I've just called it our enemy! Almost every time the Bible refers to flesh, especially in the New Testament, it's depicted as something bad. Certainly in our lives now the flesh is the enemy of the Spirit. Paul says that the mind set on the flesh is death (Romans 8:6), which doesn't really make it sound like he thinks the flesh is a good thing.

But remember: all of these verses refer to the flesh in its fallen, sinful state. It's the same with authors and pastors who call on us to crucify the flesh: they're talking about the flesh as it is now, after Eden. The flesh wasn't always as it is now.

On the sixth day of Creation, after God had made Adam and Eve, He took a look around—at the Garden, at the animals, at the plants and oceans and galaxies—and evaluated what He had done. "God saw all that He had made, and behold, it was very good" (Genesis 1:31). Notice this: Adam and Eve were included in this evaluation. Man and woman, in their physical bodies, were proclaimed *good* by God Almighty.

Indeed, the flesh *is* good. The human heart pumps more than one thousand gallons of blood per day and can run nonstop for over one hundred years without replacement parts. You won't find any mechanical pump that will do that. Your body produces the hundreds of compounds it needs to carry out chemical reactions for its thousands of functions. And it's completely automated! The chemicals replenish themselves as needed. Best of all for those recyclers among us, this vast manufacturing plant that is your flesh is powered by commonly found organic materials. It's not an alternative fuels project; it's your body.

And this only scratches the surface. We could go on for books and books about the other wonders of this miraculous creation you call your body. Consider its transportation system that allows you to move easily from a rocky beach to a cold swim. Or the central nervous system that adapts to changing environments and can create thoughts beyond the information fed into it. What about your immune systems, which detect newly encountered pathogens and adjust to counteract their invasion? Your body's mechanisms of wound healing can mend gaping wounds all by themselves.

The human creation was created smart, strong, and adaptive. It was just as God said: very good.

So What Went Wrong?

We know that something went amiss with mankind shortly after Creation. Adam and Eve violated God's command and ate the forbidden fruit. Admittedly, this has always been a little hard for me to understand. Why do I have to pay today for their sin way back then? You might have felt this way, too. And what's the big deal anyway? It was just one little rule about fruit.

Well, it is a big deal, and understanding the true nature of the flesh will help you see why. To begin to comprehend why the fateful fruit snack trashed all of mankind, let's look back to this event through the eyes of Gene Edwards, who, in *The Divine Romance*, describes God seeking to relieve His immense loneliness.[3]

Edwards says that in all God's creation every creature had a mate of its own species so none would be lonely. But there was still no one for God. How could there be? Where was there another of the species of God? So, God developed a plan to create a companion by placing a bit of Himself into man, transforming him into a new creation, literally a new species, making man a suitable mate for God Himself.

And though you may have acknowledged a hundred times the notion that you are a new creation, as I have, perhaps you have thought of it in some trite or figurative way only. But it is a profound reality that is essential to the completion of God's plan of salvation. That plan is not designed just to rid us of sin but to transform us into a species suitable to be a companion of God.

But God would not force the awesome privilege of this relationship on man, Edwards says. God wanted to be chosen. So, God gave man a free will. It would not be enough to give man a free will alone, though. There had to be something behind door #2. If His new companions were choosing only between obeying God on the one hand and nothing at all on the other hand, it wouldn't have been much of a decision. And both choices had to be appealing, too. If you're choosing between eating mud or eating chocolate, it's not much of a choice.

So, God would have to give them chocolate. Yes! God created the physical world and its allure to give man something to compare and choose between. Chocolate to taste, music to thrill the ears, wonderful things to feel, and enticing sights and smells of all kinds. The forbidden fruit, you'll recall, enticed Eve's physical senses: "When the woman saw that the tree was good for food, and that it was a delight to the eyes, and that the tree was desirable...she took from its fruit and ate" (Genesis 3:6).

To give man this choice, God created the fleshly world—and the physical component of our beings. It is not just that we needed a vehicle for our spirits to live in or an arena for us to walk around in. We could have remained in spiritual places and bodies as do God's other companions, the angels. The physical world and the flesh that lives in it were created to give us an appealing alternative to life in the Spirit with God. Man was placed right in the middle of a fleshly paradise to be given a choice: will it be God or the flesh?

Man's choice, of course, was the flesh, and the greatest sin of all time was carried out. When he took hold of the forbidden fruit, Adam rejected the control of the passionate, loving God, who longed only for a companion to be devoted to Him.

And so it is with us today. The world still appeals to the flesh, doesn't it? It is full of fleshly enticements and remains very effective at luring us away from relationship with God. Every time you choose to follow after the flesh, you recommit the original sin.

This is the essence of all sin: choosing the flesh over God. The flesh itself isn't bad—God created it good. But when we choose to let it control us, when we serve the flesh instead, that's called sin. Eating is not wrong, but gluttony is sin. Having sex in the context of marriage is not wrong, but having sex outside of marriage is sin. It is when we obey the flesh as our lord that we sin.

It's all about mastery. Paul said that while all earthly things were lawful for him, he wouldn't be mastered by anything (1

Corinthians 6:12). All of us obey something. And today, after all the millennia since Eden, there are still only two choices for whom to obey: God or our fleshly desires.

So, when we say we have sin in our lives, it is not the external fleshly behaviors that really are the sin. Those are by-products of the sin that resides where your desires originate. Paul doesn't say that the *flesh* is death and hostile to God. He says that *the mind set on the flesh* is what is death and hostile to God (Romans 8:6–7). The problem is deep inside.

This is why placing severe, legalistic restrictions on the external behaviors of the flesh can't defeat chronic sins. Some people prohibit dancing, card playing, movies, and more, hoping to fence themselves away from things that appeal to fleshly desire. But the problem isn't with the cards or the music or the films. It is the *desire* for these things, and no amount of rules will eradicate that desire. In fact, prohibitions usually have the effect of inflaming desire.

That's not to say we shouldn't be wise about where we go, what we watch, or whom we hang around with. But eventually we must realize that we can never restrict ourselves enough to kill the uncontrolled flesh within us. To bring about real and lasting defeat of sin in your life you need to get deep down to the depths of your being. And you can never do this on your own. You need God to change you on the inside, down where your love of this world originates.

If it is not already apparent that you could never change yourself, it will be in Section 2, where we see how thoroughly fleshly you and I really are.

THE TREATMENT

SECTION 2

CHAPTER 3

THE TREATMENT PLAN

HELLO again. Step back into my office. Please, sit down. Chapter one was a discussion of your symptoms, and chapter two was an overview of the illness. I've invited you back for another consultation because in this chapter I will lay out the treatment plan I'm recommending for you.

We shake hands and go to my desk. You sit anxiously across from me while I sink into my high-backed leather chair and casually flip through a few pages in your chart, gathering my thoughts. My furrowed brow tells you that all is not well. Finally I look up and give you one of my favorite lines for breaking things to my patients: "I've got some good news and some bad news."

A doctor with a flair for the dramatic. Wonderful. "Give it to me straight, doc," you say.

"All right. The bad news is that you've got a very serious disease. It's chronic and life threatening. It is a devastating infection that creeps through your body infesting one part after another, destroying your ability to function normally. Most patients never recover from it. It will slowly bring decay into your life until finally you are too weak to fight it any longer, and it consumes you. If left untreated, it will destroy not only your life but also the lives of the people you love."

Gulp. "Well, w–what's the good news?"

A smile spreads on my face. "The good news is that it's completely curable. All you need to do is follow a simple treatment plan and watch yourself move quickly to robust health."

Now you're paying attention. "That's fantastic, doc! Tell me what I have to do!"

That's the spirit. If your flesh really is in control of you in certain areas of your life—and it's the rare Christian who doesn't have *any* fleshly strongholds—there is a wonderfully potent cure. It doesn't take much from you. Indeed, most of what's required is simply that you choose to allow it to work in your life.

In this chapter I lay out the five-point treatment plan that is the key to saying goodbye to stubborn sin. It is the tool God has used to bring radical deliverance to thousands of Christians, myself included, who have been plagued by recurring struggles and stubborn sins. This is the most important chapter of the book.

The acronym I've chosen to help you remember these steps is LASTS:

L—Listen

A—Admit

S—Submit

T—Trust

S—Stand firm

Sounds Easy, Doesn't It?

"Ah, doc," you may be saying, "I've heard all this before. This is kids' stuff: repent, hang tough, say your prayers, blah, blah, blah. I thought you were going to offer me something original."

If that's what you're feeling, I can understand. Those words used in the acronym are right to the point, but they can leave victory over the flesh sounding easy, even trivial. These can sound like the same short, pat answers people get from Christianity, answers that never work.

You're right about this book offering something original. Allow me to explain what I feel is new and insightful about age-old concepts like "confess your sins." If you do not thoroughly understand why each of the five concepts is now new and different, you'll miss the whole power of the message.

Once you understand what the flesh is really like, you will see that:

- *Listening* is not identifying some superficial sin; it is hearing what deeper area of the flesh God wants dealt with.

- *Admitting* is not confessing you broke some rule; it is admitting that the flesh controls you.

- *Submitting* is not using willpower to overcome the flesh; it is looking at your two choices—the Spirit's rule and your love for the rewards of the flesh—and choosing to follow the Spirit.

- *Trusting* means giving up trust in your fleshly power to behave rightly and trusting God to do a work of sanctification.

- *Standing firm* is not a test of perseverance; it is nourishing the Spirit and starving the flesh while God works.

As you go through this book and you come to understand the flesh, you will begin to realize why all of this is true. Until then, I hope you can trust me that this isn't your usual Sunday school material. I think you will find that the sanctification experience I am describing in this book is one of the hardest things you and I will experience in this life.

In the rest of this chapter I have described each point in this healing plan. As you read it, consider going through the steps while concentrating on your stubborn sin. As you learn how to listen, listen to God for insight on your recurring sin. As you understand what it means to admit, go ahead and do so with your stronghold of sin. And so forth. Who knows? By the end of this chapter you could have victory over the flesh, a victory you thought would never be yours.

Let Him Who Has Ears to Hear, Hear (Listening)

The key to getting started is listening. Until you figure out (a) that you're serving the flesh in a certain area, and (b) what that area is, you will never rise above the struggle, sin, or stronghold that is crippling your growth and holding you back from the world-caliber Christian walk you desire in your heart of hearts.

Unfortunately, finding the real source of your problem is not always easy. Not that problems are hard to find. No way. Problems abound when you are struggling. It might seem like your life is falling apart and everything and everyone have decided to give you problems all at once.

The key to victory is finding the root problem that is tunneling through your life, sending up shoots that grow out in many different areas and cause trouble. The goal in the listening phase is to not get distracted by going around trying to pull up the weeds of sin in your life. You can spend all day trying to tear them up only to have them resurface again somewhere else, unless you get the root. Your anger, unforgiveness, lust, relationship problems, lost jobs, addictions—yes, even that lousy car that is driving you nuts—are all just the surface signs of the problem below.

So how do you find that hidden problem? The answer is easy: God is going to tell you.

Wait, don't throw the book away just yet. I promised no pat answers, but God really *is* going to tell you. In fact, He probably already has. Remember all those symptoms of struggling we talked about? The doubt, confusion, repetitive problems, and feelings of oppression are all signs that God is using His finger to put a little pressure on your life and point out the fact that there is a problem.

So He's got your attention, right? Now it is your job to listen as He tells you what He wants changed. I know you've been frustrated before with trying to hear God speaking. You listened for a voice, you've put out a fleece, you've trusted some wiser friend to tell you what God is saying, and it just hasn't worked. But it can and it will as you learn to hear His voice.

The Spirit nudge

When you accepted Christ into your life, the Holy Spirit entered your spirit and began a lifelong process of changing you into the image of Christ. All through the many times of struggling with your flesh, the Holy Spirit is there to help you overcome temptations and sinful desires by whispering His words of guidance into your spirit. Since He now indwells you, His voice is always there when you need it. The problem is you may not always hear it—or stop long enough to listen.

The notion of having to discern God's voice in your life can be a little scary. What does His voice sound like? What if I'm wrong? How will I know?

It is not as hard as you may think, however. First off, remember that God is Spirit, so He uses spiritual, not fleshly, language. God probably won't speak to you in fleshly language like a voice in your ears or even thoughts in your mind. Most often it is going to be a deep sensation in your spirit that is hard to define in fleshly terms.

A patient of mine gave one of the best descriptions of God's voice that I have heard. She had a very difficult medical problem that kept her from being able to eat. She required intravenous nutritional support for over nine months before gaining the strength to even consider the difficult surgery to fix her problem. She wrestled with the decision for a number of weeks. Finally, she returned with an answer: she wanted to undergo the surgery. She explained that she was ready for the procedure because God had given her a "nudge."

"A nudge?" I asked, somewhat skeptically.

"Yes," she explained. "I hear God's leading through a little 'nudge' deep inside. I can't really explain it beyond that. But I know that whenever I've received and followed these little nudges in the past, I've always ended up doing the right thing."

That was enough for me. I performed the operation, and the woman did far better than expected. She began eating in just a few days. This was all due to recognizing God's direction through the inaudible, but very clear voice deep inside her spirit.

When God gives you a nudge it is as if He is gently prodding you to get you moving in the right direction. Somewhere in your spirit you feel it, and when you recognize it, you really do not need words. His spiritual voice is as clear to your spirit as words are to your ears.

But what if you just can't hear God saying anything to you? Usually the problem is not that God is not speaking to us. The problem is that you are finding it difficult to hear and then listen. Often the Holy Spirit speaks to you Spirit to spirit.

Let's talk about how to put this into practice. During the listening phase get as much input as you can. Get advice from friends, pastors, and counselors. Read books and articles on the subject. Study every Scripture passage you can find.

At every step, keep your spiritual ears open for that Spirit nudge. Your spouse, your mother-in-law, your kid sister, or maybe your boss are all going to tell you their opinion on what's wrong with you, but it might just happen that, while listening to one of them, you feel a little tap on your spiritual shoulder. You might hear God saying, "Pay attention now. This person is saying what I'm trying to tell you." And it will be His voice, not theirs, directing you to the true problem. Most often the nudge comes when we're reading Scripture, so you must be in the Word deeply and often during this phase.

And sometimes God will speak to you *despite* what is being said on the surface. I can remember a time when I was feeling troubled and distracted by problems while sitting in church. While the pastor read his Scripture passage for the day, my mind was wandering. So I went past his chapter and continued to read through the subsequent chapters. And—you guessed it—a Spirit nudge got me. As I read, the Spirit said, "Here's what you need to deal with what's troubling you." The sermon for the day was completely different from what I needed to hear, but God still spoke His message to me. If you are trying to hear God, His voice will reach you. He's trying to get you to hear it, after all.

God can even speak through enemies. I generally try to steer clear of squabbling in the local medical system, but on one occasion I found myself embroiled in a debate on an issue I felt I had to speak out against, and so I did. It was quite a time of struggling in my life. Afterward, a person on the other side of the aisle said to me privately, "Well, a number of us thought you were getting rather full of yourself."

Ouch! Of course I wanted to argue. But deep inside I felt a rather strong Spirit nudge. No, make that a Spirit *shove*. I disagreed with everything the person said, including that statement, but I couldn't disagree with what the Spirit was saying in me. He was right.

One of the things that make it hard to hear God's voice is that your flesh will resist. Your first response to that little nudge might be to deny it. Deep inside you've known all along what the problem was, but it is scary to have it exposed. Your flesh is going to want to say, "What, me? No, I haven't heard God say anything. I'm fine. Everyone else is the problem!" If you are having trouble hearing God, stop resisting what He is telling you and listen.

You're probably going to find that you have several layers of fleshly control beneath the first one you come to realize you're grappling with. You'll see the surface problem right away, and you might even figure out something that may be behind it. But when you really listen to God, you're probably going to realize that you're still just scratching the surface. So, once you think you have heard God tell you the problem, keep listening for Him to reveal additional issues.

As I've mentioned, I struggled for a long time with unforgiveness. I asked God to take it away, along with all the relationship problems it caused. I prayed for forgiveness, confessed it as wrong, and used all the willpower I could muster to change, but I never did. God finally showed me that the reason I couldn't beat the unforgiveness was because unforgiveness *wasn't the problem*. The real problem was self-righteousness, an attitude buried in my flesh that allowed me to think I was just a little bit better than others. And below that was an even deeper problem—pride.

As I learned to listen, God showed me the deeper roots of sin that had caused the surface problems to develop. Dealing with those bottom-level strongholds brought healing that became evident on the surface as I became more forgiving.

How do you know when you've reached the bottom level? You know you've reached ground zero when you discover in you a sinful attitude against God. That's right: a sinful attitude that you're holding toward God. The attitude God wants you to deal with could involve a number of different aspects of your relationship with Him, but it will basically come down to one of two things. You're either feeling too good or too bad for God. This is the big secret to your stubborn sin, the radioactive waste at the bottom of the sea. Anger at God is the root of stubborn sin. It is the sin generator that will forever churn out chains of bondage, keeping you shackled to this stronghold of recurring sin.

If your struggle with sin is a result of God trying to get you to give up that "too good" attitude, you will find that at the root of it all you are feeling a little ripped off by God. This may be a foreign thought to you—something good Christians don't ever think of—but I can assure you it's crucial to let your thoughts go there.

Does part of you feel that God has done you wrong? Maybe He's given you the wrong husband or wife. Should He have given you someone more loving or more attractive or more something else? Has He given you the wrong child—or no child? Has He withheld from you the only thing you've really ever wanted? Do you feel you've done your part on something but God hasn't kept up His end of the bargain?

Adam and Eve's sin in the Garden was, at its root, their anger over a feeling that God had ripped them off. The serpent convinced Eve that God had jealously prevented her and Adam from having the fruit because He didn't want them to have something valuable: "You surely will not die! For God knows that in the day you eat from it your eyes will be opened, and you will be like God, knowing good and evil" (Genesis 3:4–5). They got mad at God for what He had withheld from them, and the flesh awoke with a vengeance.

In my struggling with unforgiveness I finally dug down and discovered buried attitudes of resentment against God for how I had remained obedient when others had not. The man who finds himself repeatedly drawn to pornography may be feeling mad at God for not giving him certain things in a wife. The businessman cheating on his taxes may find at the bottom level a feeling that God owes him something financially.

In others, God wants to deal with the fact that they feel "too bad" for a relationship with Him. Your surface stubborn sin may be that acid tongue of yours. As you listen, you may come to understand that this comes from a hidden defensiveness, and that defensiveness might be covering a deeper insecurity. That's enough layers of problems to keep the most persistent miner busy, but dig all the way to the bottom and there may be one more key level. Pay dirt. You may find that all of these layers are really arising from a secret feeling that you are simply too bad to really be loved by God. He wants you to correct that God issue and accept His love and forgiveness.

Many people continue in self-destructive sins because deep down they feel worthless and need to accept the truth about God's love and forgiveness. Their God issue is that they just don't believe God can make them a new creation, as He promised. Only after they get past all the surface issues and dig down to this critical truth will they accept the newness of life that He brings.

Maybe your stubborn sin comes to the surface in the form of guilt. You feel it every time you turn down those nice workaholics at church who want to suck you into their obsession. OK, you've gotten past it being their problem and have tried dealing with laziness and disobedience in you, but still no change. Keep digging, and you may find that your deepest problem is a private belief that God just hasn't gifted you as He has others in the church. You're just not good enough. He wants you to dig into relationship with Him and find what unique talents He blessed you with to make you an integral part of His body.

In your listening, keep listening. Keep digging deeper and deeper until you reach the God level. When you finally come to see that you've harbored wrong attitudes toward God, that's when you know you've found the real problem.

One note: not every sin will have anger at God as its direct cause. If you truly listen and act on what God shows you—even if it's not at "the God level"—then go your way rejoicing. But if time passes and the power of this sin has not been broken, go back to listening, and concentrate on the God level.

"It Wasn't Me!" (Admitting)

I always enjoy the *Family Circus* cartoon in the newspaper when the mother asks her kids, "Who made this mess?", and the kids all respond together, "Not me!"—as a mythical little creature with a name tag reading Not Me on his chest runs out of the room snickering. I guess I found it funny because we had that same creature living in our house when the kids were young. What a perfect picture of the tenacity of the human spirit. We can be caught dead to rights, guilty as sin, with our hand still in the cookie jar, and still deny we did anything wrong.

It is exactly this tenacity that keeps us from finding freedom from the stubborn sins that plague us in life. We hate the situation we find ourselves in, and yet we defend it. Let's say you've been through the listening phase and you now know what lies at the root of this pattern you keep repeating, this fleshly traffic circle you can never seem to exit. That's wonderful that you know what it is. But if you are ever going to change, you need to admit, without any excuses, that the way you are right now is wrong.

Just think about it: you can't change directions in life, whether it is going north on the highway instead of south, changing jobs, or turning from sin, until you first admit that the way you were going is wrong. It is a universal law. All human change begins with stopping your progress and changing your direction. The theological word for it is *repentance.*

So, after you have listened to God's voice and identified the area in your flesh that needs to be corrected, the next step is to admit that it is wrong and repent. Sounds pretty basic right? Christianity 101. Before coming to Christ your life may have consisted of sex, drugs, and rock 'n roll. You woke up one too many times in the wrong bed and decided you were headed for destruction. You repented. God forgave you. You moved on. Now that you're a Christian, you may have thought all that would be behind you, but you find there is still sin in your life. So what do you do? You repent. Do the rotten behavior again. Repent. Do it again. Repent. Do it again.

Why are you still struggling after repenting of your besetting sin a thousand times? Doesn't the Bible promise that where the Spirit of God is, there is freedom? So why aren't you free of this? The answer is that you're no longer in Christianity 101. You've advanced to higher education in your spiritual life, and it's time to take repentance to a level beyond just admitting you've done a bad thing.

Now you are left with the really hard sin issues. The sins you committed before you were a Christian, those things you did just to fill the void left by not knowing God, fall away pretty easily when He comes in and fills your life with love and purpose. After salvation, the sins that remain are those that are more deeply rooted in your fallen human nature. These are the tough ones. They arise out of who you are deep inside. And, as you are going to see in the upcoming chapters, *who you are* is someone completely engulfed in the flesh, even if you are a Christian.

So it's not going to be as easy as just saying "I'm sorry" for those surface behaviors that continue to bother you. It is not being a bad boy or girl that God is concerned about now. There is a much bigger offense occurring deep inside you. Somewhere in your life you have given control to the flesh. When the flesh is in control of you, God is not. That's called sin. There is raging inside of every Christian an ongoing battle for his or her allegiance. *The definition of sin is allowing the flesh to control your actions.*

Once you've listened to God and discovered what area of flesh controls you, it is time to 'fess up. It's great to know that you keep stealing because you're mad at God for giving you a mother who sold all your favorite toys when you were four, but if you don't confess that those inner feelings are controlling you, the flesh's power will not be broken.

This isn't as easy as it sounds. Believe it or not, we all tend to hold on to our favorite fleshly activities and attitudes *even when we know they're sin*. Even when they're destroying us and those around us.

Smoking is a great example. You can tell smokers over and over that smoking is bad, but still they do it. They are sticking a loaded gun in their mouth and making excuses for why it's all right. "I'll gain weight if I quit," or "I don't smoke that much." Often they say, "I had a grandfather who smoked, and he lived to be eighty!" I wish I had a dollar for every time I've heard that one. They don't change because they aren't really convinced it is wrong—or they like what it does for them more than they dislike what it does *to* them.

When the first heart attack or lung nodule comes along, suddenly the story changes. People who never could quit suddenly drop the habit overnight. Why? Because now they are convinced.

The withering work of God

Sometimes we need convincing, too. As we will see, the flesh loves the stubborn sin in your life, and it will not willingly let go. And sometimes we help the problem because we're not altogether sure it's that big a deal. If that's you, I've got some news: God is going to help you become convinced.

Some of that convincing is going to come through an inner work of the Holy Spirit. Remember, He's alive inside you and promises that He's not going to just hang out in your spirit. He's going to let that new life in the spirit spread out and transform your mortal body as well (see Romans 8:10–11), and that means sanctifying your flesh. It would be nice if, every time He brings conviction, you and I would accept His instruction, repent, get an A for the course, and get to move on. Unfortunately, with the more stubborn sins we are dealing with here, it is usually not this easy.

When your flesh is holding you in bondage, the Holy Spirit has other means to help you come to a place of being able to admit where you need to get your flesh under control.

He will send along something that will open your eyes to how bad your sin really is. It may not be literally sent by God: it could be a car wreck or a close call with an affair. If it gets your attention about your sin, it's something God is using to try to get through to you. All He has to do is just allow your fleshly area of bondage to progress to its logical destination, because problems will automatically result.

The pain He allows is lovingly designed to help you see the depravity of your sin. All the while, you're praying, "God, take this bad habit away from me; it's making me feel bad." But God is saying *no* because He wants you to see how bad the sin you're clinging to really is.

This is not just about feeling bad as a result of bad circumstances. This is a supernatural work of the Holy Spirit to bring pressure on your life, from inside you and from the outside, to expose the sin and bring conviction. This is the reality behind Romans 8. It's not always a nice, free-flowing experience of walking the aisle after a stirring sermon. In fact, with the stubborn sins, it never is. As the life of Christ spreads out into your mortal body and confronts these fleshly strongholds, it is more like throwing ice into a vat of hot oil. Your life may feel like an eruption of spattering turmoil until the flesh is subdued.

When I was struggling with unforgiveness, I prayed, "God, cleanse me of unforgiveness because it's hurting my marriage." But I was really holding on to the self-righteousness buried in my flesh. I didn't like the conflict it caused in our relationship, but I secretly did like the feeling of superiority it gave me deep inside. And so God sent severe struggling as the wake-up call. As a result of these tough times, I finally glimpsed how ugly my self-righteousness was and how badly it was hurting others. When I understood that, it wasn't so fun to hold on to anymore. Seeing this allowed me to fully repent and begin the process of changing from the inside out.

God is doing the same for you. Times of trouble are the gust of hot wind He uses to cause our flesh to wither so that we see its pathetic weakness and our sin's awful ugliness and turn instead to the eternal. Nineteenth-century preacher Charles Spurgeon describes this process as "the withering work of the Spirit":

> The Spirit blows upon the flesh, and that which seems vigorous becomes weak. That which was fair to look upon is smitten with decay, and the true nature of the flesh is discovered. Its deceit is laid bare, and its power is destroyed. There is space for the dispensation of the ever-abiding Word and for the rule of the Great Shepherd whose words are spirit and life.[1]

So don't ask God to remove your struggles just yet. Pray during this time that God will show you how ugly and harmful your sin really is, and how it is keeping you from Him. Until you are fully convinced of that, you cannot and will not fully repent. But when true repentance occurs, the floodgates of grace burst open, releasing God's healing power into your life.

Doing good in the power of the flesh

Here's some graduate-level course material in repentance: you may also have to repent of what you do right. Notice an interesting facet to my definition that sin is whenever the flesh controls you: even good things done under the control of the flesh are sin. As important as it is to confess to God everything you've done wrong, it is equally important to admit some of what you did right if it was done in the power of the flesh.

Sound ridiculous? A few years ago I would have thought so, too. That was before the Lord revealed to me the message of Philippians 3, where Paul lists all of his fleshly accomplishments:

> If anyone else has a mind to put confidence in the flesh, I far more: circumcised the eighth day, of the nation of Israel, of the tribe of Benjamin, a Hebrew of Hebrews; as to the Law, a Pharisee; as to zeal, a persecutor of the church; as to the righteousness which is in the Law, found blameless.
> —PHILIPPIANS 3:4–6

At the end of the passage he tells us what his fleshly works amounted to: dross, refuse, or (how shall I say this delicately?) poop (v. 8). You get the point. It's not good.

A friend of mine used to lift his hands in praise and worship, but he no longer does. While I believe such an expression of worship is a very good thing, for him it was right to stop. Why? Well, he'd just gone through the teachings contained in this book, and he suddenly realized that this good thing he was doing in worship was actually a sin for him. He told me that he was standing there in worship, when suddenly conviction came into his heart: "Why are you lifting your hands? You don't do that when you're alone with Me."

My friend realized that he wasn't lifting his hands to worship Jesus Christ but to show the people in the congregation how righteous he was. He was doing a good thing—something we're even instructed to do in 1 Timothy 2:8—but in his case at that point in his life it was a fleshly activity designed to bring him, not God, glory and honor, so it needed to be purified.

What about you? Are you doing any good things for bad reasons? Rushing to perform certain activities to be thought well of by someone you're trying to curry favor with? Trying to be seen as a certain kind of person or receive a fleshly reward? The Bible tells us that God knows our motives (1 Samuel 16:7), and that whatever is not done "from faith" is sin (Romans 14:23).

If God has shown you that the flesh is controlling you in some area, even a "good" thing, don't defend it, hide it, or coddle it. Admit it. If the flesh is in control at *any* point, you need to repent in order to find change that lasts.

Choose You This Day Whom You Will Serve (Submitting)

Sin has a way of sneaking up on you, doesn't it? You're just strolling along in your spiritual life with everything going pretty well. You're enjoying your devotions. Your prayer life is consistent and powerful. You were just elected deacon at church. You seem to have so many answers in life that you're starting to think about writing a book.

Then suddenly it happens. That friend from the bad old days calls you out of the blue and wants to go out. Pornographic spam e-mail arrives. Or your brother-in-law decides to start pushing your buttons at a family get-together. Whatever it is, for you it is the same old problem, and it's back for another round in what seems to be an endless boxing match with sin.

But not to worry: this time you're ready for it. You've already been through the listening phase and have identified the problem, and you've even admitted it as sin. You're not out of it yet, though. You still have a choice to make. God has presented His preferred course of action for you: letting Him rule you in this area. But now the flesh presents its candidate: the opportunity to go back into that old sin. The polls open up, and the Nation of You awaits the crucial swing vote.

Until now, you haven't even been able to choose. You've just been giving in to the flesh's control in this area. That's why it's a stubborn sin—it won't go away, and you can never seem to gain victory over it. But now you know its name (through listening) and have confessed it before God. Reaching this plateau doesn't mean the flesh won't bother you anymore. What it means is that the power to choose is finally in your hands.

Submitting means using your will to choose God's way over the way of the flesh. We actually have very little to do in this battle with sin. We can't overcome the power of the flesh through willpower. But we *can* choose whether we're going to submit to God's power or to the power of the flesh. Imagine a large boulder delicately balanced. With the gentlest of shoves you can send it rolling down the hillside in one of two directions. What you do at this moment of choice will have far-reaching ramifications.

Making an act of the will to submit yourself to God's sovereignty at this critical juncture is going to release the power of the Holy Spirit to bring about changes deep inside you. You send the boulder tumbling down God's preferred way, and He'll take care of what happens next. It was the same way in salvation, after all. Just as your act of will to surrender to God was how you began your journey with Christ, so also these daily acts of will to surrender to God is how you live the Christian life (Galatians 3:3).

This is how God addresses the deeper, more difficult areas of bondage in your flesh. These issues take more time, and you may not be able to make the right choices to change your behavior right away after submitting them to God's control. When you begin submitting your problem area to God, you may only have enough strength to recognize you have a choice before seeing yourself once again make the wrong choice. But it's a start.

These areas will change, however, as God's power continues to sanctify you from the inside out. As you truly submit these areas and God's sanctifying power goes to work, you will notice your desire for the sins of the flesh will weaken and fade.

Laps in the wilderness

If you're having trouble submitting an area of your flesh to God, He is going to help you once again. Just as with admitting, though, God is not going to force you to submit to Him. One thing God will not do is override your will. God will not steal away the fleshly things that you hold on to. Neither will He remove the struggles that they produce in your life. You cannot go on with Him into freedom while you hold on to the flesh. You also cannot really go back. Once you have committed your life to God and He has begun the work of sanctification in your life, it's going to continue. God promises to complete that work in you (Philippians 1:6).

So if you cannot go forward and you cannot go back, there is only one thing to do—wander in circles. This is exactly what happens in your times of struggling. To help you want to let go of your area of recurring sin, God is going to give you a little vacation—in the wilderness. Your troubles will pile up because you are wandering in circles. God is giving you one opportunity after another to choose to submit the area of unsanctified flesh to Him until you are finally ready to give it up.

The Israelites in the wilderness are the textbook example of this. After God freed them from Egypt, God sent a little discomfort into their lives to get their attention. The Egyptian army was following them. That was God's little Spirit nudge to get them to deal with their lack of trust.

Unfortunately, with the distraction of thousands of Egyptian warriors on their tail, they missed that nudge. Their response was, "Is it because there were no graves in Egypt that you have taken us away to die in the wilderness?" (Exodus 14:11). They chose to grumble against God rather than listen to Him to identify their problem. Their discomfort was temporarily relieved when God flushed the Egyptian army in the Red Sea, but afterward He sent them right back to the wilderness to try again.

The next bit of discomfort was a lack of water, and again God was alerting them to their underlying trust problem. Again they were given the choice to examine themselves or make up some excuse for why it wasn't their problem. They went with plan B and decided this time it was Moses' fault. So, what did God do? Sent them back to the wilderness! Next they struggled with a lack of food. Would they choose to follow God? Not yet. Instead of seeing God's purpose in their struggles, they again blamed God. Back to the wilderness!

They did more laps through the wilderness than the Sinai track team. This continued until Israel reached the edge of Canaan. Now they grappled with trusting God in the face of giants inhabiting the Promised Land. This time they really gave up on God's way. They actually wanted to dump Moses and return to Egypt.

Can you imagine choosing to return to slavery rather than submitting to God and going into the land flowing with milk and honey? Unfortunately, this is the same choice we make as we cling to the flesh and avoid the sanctification process God is trying to accomplish in us. We choose to return to being slaves to our fleshly bondages rather than move on with God. God's response: back to the wilderness!

This is why there seems to be no cure for your struggles at times. It is not because God is unable or unwilling to heal you. *It is because you cling to the flesh that binds you.* Every time you decide to hold on to the flesh rather than listen to God, He sends you for one more lap in the wilderness of struggling to help loosen your grip on the flesh.

If you have tried and failed repeatedly to submit an area of your life to God, pray that He will help you let it go. Watchman Nee suggests the following prayer when faced with this difficult problem:

> If you find you in your own strength cannot let them [things you need to surrender to God] go, then realize that you can overcome if you are willing to tell God, "O God, I commit to You what I cannot let go of. Please work in me till I am willing to let go."[2]

A part of the Hebrew nation was controlled by the Spirit and followed God in the wilderness. Another part was under the control of the flesh. The flesh-dominated part was holding the entire nation back from spiritual progress. So God turned up the heat in the wilderness, and a whole generation of people who would not submit to God was destroyed.

The anguish you feel inside as you battle your repetitive problem is the result of God's work destroying the flesh that controls you. If there is an area of flesh that you cannot or will not submit, He will turn up the heat in your life and kill it so it will no longer hold you back spiritually. This is all part of His treatment plan for freeing you from the flesh.

Perhaps this is not the peace, joy, and victory that you've heard about finding in Christianity, but it is the way to your promised land. If you continue to choose God during this process, He will systematically defeat the flesh's control in your life and give you victory. Keep calling out to Him in these difficult times. Don't give up, and He will bring you through the wilderness to a place where you are free of the bondage of the flesh and ready to move on with Him.

"You Take It From Here, Lord" (Trusting)

I was ten years old. I was standing on the edge of the high dive at the community pool, feeling as frightened as if I were about to jump out of an airplane, except I had no parachute. It was the highest diving board at the pool, and though it stood only ten feet off the surface of the water, it was plenty high enough to give an exhilarating freefall to any who would venture up its high steps and dare to leap off. Or so I'd heard.

So far I had not dared. More than once I had climbed the slippery, wet ladder to creep out to the edge of the board and peek over the edge to gaze in fear at the water that seemed a mile below my feet. Standing at the edge I felt the wind blow a cool chill over my body, and I sensed the thrill I would find if only I could bring myself to take one simple step beyond the edge of the board. But I could not. Every time, I went back and climbed down the ladder in defeat.

One day, I decided I would wait for courage no longer. It would take no great skill, I knew. I wasn't planning to win an Olympic diving medal. I needed only to jump. I could do it. I knew I could. Today was the day. I climbed the perilous ladder one more time and walked cautiously but determinedly to the end of the board. I was ready. I had chosen. Then I took one step forward and placed myself completely in the hands of gravity.

The next few seconds were a rush of spinning thoughts and swirling sensations as I realized I'd made the metamorphosis from scared child to courageous high-diver. Even as I splashed into the water I knew I would never again be afraid of the high dive. I ran back to the bottom of the steps to jump again and again. The issue of the high dive was defeated once and for all.

In that leap, I made only one small decision, and gravity took care of the rest. Gravity has a 100 percent effectiveness rate. What is given into its power *will* be drawn downward. So it is in our battle with the flesh. We have only a small decision to make (submitting), and then God—who has a better effectiveness record even than gravity—will bring about the right results. We don't have to help Him or remind Him, any more than I had to remind gravity to seize me once I stepped off the board. If you choose to submit your will to God's power, He will work sanctification into that part of your life.

"Help my unbelief!"

In the midst of struggle I used to pray, "God, give me the strength to change!" Sounds pretty good, right? But this is a wrong prayer! This is the prayer of a "doer," a person who wants God to give *him* the power so that *he* can fix the problem by *himself*. This prayer never helped me, and it probably won't help you. God does not want to give you power so that you can change your actions. He wants to send *His* power into your life and change you Himself.

But then again you've heard the old adage "Just have faith" before, haven't you? Me, too. Easier said than done, right? Well, remember that it takes only a little faith to get started. A mustard seed's worth of faith will do. This is all the faith Christ required to heal a possessed child. When the child's father implored Christ to heal his son, Christ replied, "All things are possible to him who believes." In anguish the father cried out, "I do believe; help my unbelief!" (Mark 9:24), and the child was healed. God is not offended when we say, "Lord, I only have a little faith; give me some more!"

It's possible to get stuck in this phase. If you really have no faith that God is going to change you, you will be stalled here for some time. But there is still hope for you. Recognize that your lack of faith in God—and especially its opposite truth: your reliance on the flesh—is itself sin. Go back to the admitting phase and confess your lack of faith as sin, and ask God to begin effecting change by cleansing that out of you.

I reached this distressing point in my life when I was struggling with some deeply rooted fleshly attitudes. Nothing seemed to help. I knew precisely what area God was working on, but nothing I did brought change. Even reading Scripture brought no comfort or direction. The truths were all there, but they were not true in my life. It only frustrated me to read them again. I remember crying out to God, "If these things are really true, then make them happen in my life!" The more I prayed this way, the more frustrated I became, so I stopped praying.

Eventually, I grew tired of being miserable; I gave up praying that God would fix my surface problems, and I confessed my lack of faith. This took me right down to the God issue at the foundation of my problem. It came down to trusting Him or not. Starting with this very fundamental question, God rebuilt my faith from the bottom up.

Very soon afterward I was so impacted that I decided to be re-baptized. I wanted to profess that finally I really believed in God's power in a way that I hadn't before. My walk with Him grew by leaps and bounds. I developed a whole new understanding of how He works in our lives and how magnificent His grace is.

Oh, that problem that was making me struggle? It was fixed, too. By that point the little surface problem seemed trivial. When the whole iceberg of hidden sin melted away, that little portion of it that stuck out of the top of my life hardly mattered anymore. It just disappeared as God produced change from the inside out. And so will yours when you give up trying to fix that little problem on the surface and trust God to go to work underneath.

God gives us an amazing promise in 1 John 5. He tells us that there is one kind of prayer God will always grant, one category of petition in which He will always give us what we ask for. See if you can spot it:

> This is the confidence which we have before Him, that, if we ask anything according to His will, He hears us. And if we know that He hears us in whatever we ask, we know that we have the requests which we have asked from Him.
> —1 John 5:14–15

In other words, if we ask God to give us something He already wants to give us, it's a slam dunk. We know it's God's will to sanctify us, right? Scripture says so. So if we ask Him to take up sovereignty in this area, we can know without doubt that He will do so because it's His will. He loves it when we ask Him to do for us exactly what He wants to do for us! Once you've found the thing inside you that has been causing your stubborn sin, and you have confessed it as sin and asked God to rule in it, you can rest assured that He will.

The War of Attrition (Standing Firm)

Because Sherry had been raised in a Christian home, she knew all about sin and repentance and trusting God to cleanse her. But none of that had prevented her from landing in one failed relationship after another. It was hard as a young adult to be shackled to one loser after another, but that was kid stuff compared to the problems she found herself in lately.

It all seemed to start after the first sexual relationship led to the first marriage. Short-lived as it was, it left her with a child to raise and a load of guilt and hurt. It took months—years, really—to get to the point where she could get her head cleared enough to start searching for God's way and leaning on Him for answers. She examined her situation, discovered her failures, and confessed them to God. But just as quickly as she did, along came loser #27, promising an easier way without all that religious stuff.

It took another year or two to figure out he was a dead end, but the truth of God seemed no clearer. Now there was another baby and another failed relationship. The weight of bills and child care made it even easier for her to believe that the next wolf in sheep's clothing would be her savior—and the cycle repeated, with occasional brief interludes of trying to follow God's way. But more years passed, more relationships ended, and the pile of hurt and confusion grew into a mountain.

If you feel like Sherry, and your problems are getting harder, not easier, though you are choosing to open yourself to God's sanctification, keep in mind that there are some problems in life that are so deeply rooted in our flesh that they are not eliminated overnight. For Sherry, it was relationships. For you, it might be something else. In fact, you may find that the longer you are a Christian, the harder life gets. This is because the easier problems have been dealt with, leaving only the toughest ones to fight. These sins are so deeply ingrained in us that only the slow grinding of God's persistent Spirit will finally wipe them out. That's what *standing firm* is all about.

Dealing with these issues first requires standing firm in the process of sanctification. Maybe the first pass through the LASTS cycle hasn't eliminated every problem, but don't give up. There may be more God wants to work in you; perhaps His work is in process but not completed. Go back and listen for areas of your flesh that may still be in control, admit them, and trust in God for His cleansing work.

Note that LASTS is not a one-way journey but a cycle. We must travel the LASTS pathway whenever we encounter recurring patterns of fleshliness in our lives, following it through to that destination where that part of our flesh is in obedience to God's Spirit. But we have to remain ever vigilant against a new pattern arising. Sanctification continues throughout our lives. When we allow God to have lordship over one area of our flesh, He will move on to the next. Keep an eye out for new patterns of situations, feedback, and struggles. Then go back to the listening phase and pray for ears to hear.

And remember, you may not have found the root of your sin until you've reached the God issue. Sherry dealt with a lot of sexual sin, and then she had to go back and deal with a cycle of resentment and hurt. She wasn't done dealing with her area of struggle, however, until she got down to her underlying lack of trust in God to care for her that made her cling to men. Keep digging until your search for fleshly bondages takes you back to God.

Standing firm also requires standing on truth. The father of lies doesn't want you to be sanctified. He's morally opposed to it. God has shown you what your problem is by this point, so Satan says the opposite to get you to give up. God says you need to submit your lust; Satan says God just doesn't want you to have fun. God says your old friends are pulling you away; Satan tells you not to worry, maybe you can witness to them. Don't believe the lies that don't match up with the truth in God's Word.

Just as your search for sin in your life leads back to a God issue, the lies lead back to God as well. Satan will tell you that you are struggling because God has forsaken you, not because He is doing a work of sanctification. Perhaps he may tell you that you have gotten in over your head in this problem and fallen too far away from God, and God cannot help you. Don't believe these lies. Stand firm on the truth of God's Word that He is sovereign (Daniel 4:35), is in control of everything that happens to you, loves you like a father (Luke 11:11–13), and has only your best interest in mind.

The war of attrition

Standing firm against these deeply rooted problems, with Satan pounding on your head with lies, can be tough. It can take a long time to root them out. Defeating these entrenched problems will require fighting a war of attrition.

This is a military tactic in which one army tries to defeat an enemy army by slowly whittling it down. Often it was done by surrounding an enemy and starving them out. Imagine a battle in which an army surrounds an enemy fortress and then simply waits. The besieging army doesn't have to attack at all. It's resting, free to move around, and receiving supplies. The besieged, on the other hand, are in trouble. Their supply lines are cut off, and they cannot escape. Every day that passes makes them a little hungrier, a little weaker, and a little more desperate.

This type of warfare does not require new fighting techniques or weapons. It simply requires *standing firm* in siege against the foe. It takes time, but it is sometimes the only way to conquer a difficult, strongly entrenched enemy.

To win the war of attrition against your fleshly stronghold you need to cut off the supply lines that strengthen your flesh. This means turning off the TV, staying away from worldly friends, and avoiding anything else that feeds your flesh—especially in the area where you are struggling. This might mean staying away from that person who always sets you off, or even stopping your involvement in ministry if it has been a fleshly pursuit.

I said earlier that prohibiting dancing and card playing wouldn't stamp out the flesh, yet here I seem to be contradicting that. But I'm not: no amount of rules or restrictions *by themselves* can eradicate flesh. But if you're avoiding certain things to cut off your flesh's ability to resist you, it's a good thing. Examine your fleshly stronghold to find where it gets its strength, and then cut the supply lines that feed it.

You also want to strengthen yourself against the fleshly enemy. This is where the spiritual disciplines come in. Things like prayer, fellowship, worship, and Scripture reading are not just religious rituals. They are fortifications and supplies that will strengthen you as the enemy weakens. In your darkest times of struggling, it is often tough to pray and worship. When you're hurting, Christians are sometimes the last people you want to be around, but get to church anyway. You need the spiritual nutrition to sustain you in your battle.

As you stand firm in your long war of attrition against the most stubborn areas of sin, another important source of strength is, honestly, real medical care. As we will see in the following chapters, the flesh is thoroughly linked to our physical bodies. Physical ailments can produce significant struggles in your life and may be benefited by medical intervention.

The best place to start is to remember some basic health recommendations. Eating right, exercising, and getting good sleep are important parts of winning the war of attrition raging inside you. Your enemy is trying to wear you down by keeping you strung out on stress, eating junk food on the fly, and crashing in bed at 1:00 a.m. every night. Fight back by keeping yourself physically strong and able to keep fighting.

Medical problems such as narcolepsy or insomnia, PMS, thyroid hormone imbalance, chronic exposure to the stress-related hormones adrenaline and corticosteroids, and emotional illness can all produce significant problems in a person's life. Ongoing illness such as pain syndromes, chronic intestinal problems, obesity, or any long-standing illness can also place a significant amount of stress on a person's life, leading to a variety of struggles.

If physical problems are causing your struggling, then by all means go see a doctor for help. God has blessed us with a wealth of knowledge about how we can use physical principles to benefit our lives. While standing firm, go back to the listening phase of sanctification and consider that God may be leading you to deal with some medical issues.

Keep in mind, however, that the physical ailment may actually be the surface discomfort that God is using to get you to deal with deeper issues. Covering up spiritual problems with medication would be like giving pain pills to someone with appendicitis. You may feel better for a little while, but eventually the problem inside is going to rupture, and you'll be worse off in the end. So even as you seek help from human physicians, keep in mind that medical help is only one additional resource to be considered while undergoing God's treatment plan. Your life and healing are in the hands of the Great Physician, not any fleshly physician.

Winning the war of attrition requires simply standing firm in your resolve to eliminate the enemy once you have it surrounded. The only way you can lose is to give up and walk away, to open up your battle lines and let the surrounded foe escape to again ravage the countryside. While giving up sounds foolish at this point, it is a strong temptation. You may feel you've made progress in so many areas, but in this one you just can't seem to gain the upper hand. You continue to succumb to the temptations in one certain area.

You may even fall deeply into sin again.

Relapse

If this war of attrition on a certain area of sin drags on for months or even years, it becomes very draining. This is what is happening in times of prolonged struggling. God is starving out the deepest stronghold of flesh remaining in you. The pressure, confusion, loneliness, and oppression that accompany struggling are draining your flesh of its strength, weakening its hold on your life.

But it can feel as if you're not making any headway at all. Maybe you have a relapse—you plunge into an episode of awful sin—and you feel you're just as full of sin and just as chained to the sin as ever. Don't believe it! It's a lie. The enemy can't break your lines by force, so he'll try to do it by treachery. A wild animal always fights fiercest when its back is to the wall.

In such times it may be helpful to compare your situation now with what things were like before you began this process. Maybe it's something as crass as counting how many days or weeks it's been since you last gave in to the sin. A man who struggles to be free of pornography might give in to it once again, but if after his confession before God he discovers that it has actually been three months since his last fall, it might encourage him. If a woman lets slip a catty remark about someone she used to have nothing but ill will toward, perhaps she would be encouraged to see that she's actually had a number of conversations about this woman in which she didn't say anything negative.

Sanctification is a process. That means that an area that was once 100 percent given over to the flesh may now, thanks perhaps to the LASTS treatment plan, have only a 20 percent hold over you. But that means that there is still a 20 percent chance that you may choose to give in to it every time the polls go open—which might be multiple times every day. If you've ever had your picnic ruined on a day that had only a 20 percent chance of rain, you know that it's still possible.

If you relapse, confess the sin and then go back to the listening phase. Begin the LASTS pathway again. But notice that you're not starting over with sanctification. That's still in process, and God has made much headway in you. Every time you yield to Him, it's a setback for the enemy. So the bad guy scored a victory on you? So what? You're still the besieger, and he's still the besieged.

When you find yourself ready to collapse in exhaustion, it is then that you are nearest victory—because exhaustion is the goal. God is draining you of any energy in your flesh so that you become reliant on God's strength in your spirit. So no matter how much you may want to give up, stand firm!

Up on the Exam Table With You

Well, how are you doing so far? Intrigued? Enlightened? Hopeful? In this chapter I've talked about the theory behind bringing the flesh under the authority of God's Spirit. For the rest of the book we'll be looking at the nuts and bolts of how it happens.

As a physician, I have been taught about every chemical, physical, anatomical, circulatory, autonomic, and even electrical system in the human body. As a Christian, I have been trained in matters pertaining to the Bible and walking with Jesus Christ. As a *Christian physician*, I have a unique vantage point, a wonderful perspective of medicine that I can bring to my study of God's Word—and a spiritual understanding that I can bring to my study of human physiology. It is the marriage of these two perspectives, infused with God's intervention in my mind and experience, that has brought about the unique teaching of this book.

In the following chapters I will take you through the physiological systems of the body. As we do, understand that this is not just trivia you don't really need to know. What I'll be telling you is precisely what you need to know about how the body works *to understand how the flesh works.* To truly know your enemy and comprehend what you're grappling with, you must understand the physiological side of the flesh.

When I talk about homeostasis, for instance, it's not just so you can impress your spouse with a five-dollar word. It's so you can detect precisely how the flesh may be ruling you in that arena of your life. As you come to understand reflexes, you'll come to see how the flesh benefits from decisions that no longer pass through the analysis center of your brain. With each chapter your mastery of exactly how the flesh works in your life—usurping even the body God created as good in the Garden—will grow. And with knowledge comes power.

At the end of every chapter in Section 2 I will take you through the LASTS sequence for the physiological system we've studied in that chapter. My hunch is that you'll find your stubborn sin in the next few pages—maybe not by what words and examples I've chosen, but as the Holy Spirit works through these printed words to give you those *Aha!* insights into why you or someone you love has not been able to get beyond a particular recurring sin.

Whenever you go to the doctor, you know you may have to endure a little poking and prodding. This doctor's visit is no different. Don't be surprised if during this examination process you feel a little vulnerable and maybe even uncomfortable. It is all part of the process of investigating your life to discover your problem.

So it's time for you to jump up on the exam table. Read on, my good patient, and discover how to bring the flesh under the control of God's Spirit, one physiological system at a time.

CHAPTER 4

HOMEOSTASIS— DEFENDING YOUR STEADY STATE

REMEMBER Todd and Becky from way back in chapter one? Todd's the one who struggles with pornography, and Becky can't seem to get past her bitterness toward her brother. Let's come back to them now.

Todd is at the mall with his wife, shopping. Actually, she's shopping; he's just along to flash the plastic and carry the bags. They round a corner in the crowded mall, and, right in front of him, Todd sees a beautiful young woman headed right toward him. Her cut-off T-shirt clings to every curve and leaves her solid abs on display—including a belly button ring to emphasize the point. Her low-rise jeans reveal the top of her pelvis and tempt his mind to imagine the rest.

At first, the sight of her is a shock. He wasn't expecting to get an eyeful of this. But now that he sees her, Todd decides he'd really like to look at her very closely. He gives no resistance to the temptation to drink it all in. And so as they walk past each other, he stares at the woman for as long as he can without breaking his neck. Wow.

Finally he turns back front—and notices his wife looking at him, an angry sneer on her face.

"What were you doing?" she asks.

"Hmm?"

"Don't play dumb. I saw you ogling that woman. Why don't you just go after her, huh? Follow her all over the mall like some kind of stalker. Fine with me. I know you'd rather look at her than me anyway. You can find your own way home. I'm leaving."

Uh, oh.

Todd feels threatened, ashamed, and angry all at once. "You can't go. I've got the keys. And so what if I like to look at beautiful women? It's not like I'm sleeping with her or anything. I can shop all I want, so long as I don't buy."

And so it goes.

Now let's check in on Becky. She's on the phone with her mom talking about Thanksgiving plans. During the conversation her mother lets out that Rick, Becky's brother, is going to be staying with them for the holiday.

"What? Mom, make him get a hotel. It's not like he's poor."

"Becky, of course he'll stay with us. He always does."

"I know, Mom. Did you ever think that maybe *I* might want to stay at the house sometime? Why is it always him?"

"You're talking nonsense, Becky. Why would you need to stay with us—you only live ten miles away!"

"Oh, that's great. Now I'm talking nonsense?"

"Becky, calm down. Why do you always get like this whenever we talk about Rick?"

"I don't always get like this, Mom. What does that even mean? Get like what?"

"You get so angry."

"I'm not angry, Mom, OK? Why are you always hassling me about it anyway?"

Time Out

Oh, boy, did you see that? Todd and Becky are both a little out of control here. What set them off? How did it escalate like that?

These examples give a good picture of how one powerful part of your flesh works. They also show how the same process can come out in people with different surface problems. You can easily spot the surface problems of unforgiveness and lust. In this chapter I'm going to show you how to examine situations like this so you can learn to spot where the underlying flesh problem lies in Todd and Becky—and maybe in you, too. I hope you can insert your own stubborn flesh behavior into this discussion.

HOMEOSTASIS—DEFENDING YOUR STEADY STATE

YOUR BASIC WIRING

First, we're going to start with a little basic physiology.

Wait! Don't turn the page and skip on to the chapter that you think has your problem in it. You're going to need to understand this stuff to get all the rest of it. And don't worry; I've kept it pretty simple. And I promise to give you the bare minimum of what you need to know to understand and defeat your flesh. If you are a medical type who wants to say, "Hey, there's more to it than that," I hope you'll forgive any oversimplification.

Let's start with your basic wiring. All the organ systems in your body are interconnected through a marvelous network of nerve fibers. I need to take a minute here to explain these pathways so you'll be able to understand all the fleshly processes we will discuss throughout Section 2.

Your brain's main purpose in life is to make sure all of your organ systems are working right and integrating well to maintain your general health and well-being. To do so it has to keep track of everything that goes on inside and outside of your body, and decide the best way to deal with it all. The way it does this is exceedingly complex, but happily it can all be boiled down to one basic process, with three distinct parts:

1. Receiving a stimulus
2. Analyzing it
3. Responding to it

It goes like this. Sensory receptors in your body (like your eyes) send messages to your brain: "Hey, I'm picking something up here." Then the neurons in your brain analyze the information and decide what to do about it. "Ow! It's the sun, and it's too bright! Blot that thing out before I go blind." Your brain sends a signal back out into the body with instructions to respond to the stimulus. "Hey, arm, make yourself useful and block that sun for me, would you?" Up the arm lifts and, *voilà*, problem solved.

This process and the wiring in your body that make it possible are known as a *neurologic pathway*. Neurologic pathways are responsible for producing every response your body makes. Something stinks, so you hold your nose. You're late for class, so you

Say Goodbye to Stubborn Sin

run faster. You don't like that song, so you skip to the next one.

In the receiving part of this process, every aspect of your internal and external world is monitored by your body's ten million sensory input fibers. Changes in temperature, blood pressure, even the concentration of chemicals in your blood are watched in this way. Your emotional state is monitored by this system, too, and perceived threats are sensed so that responses can be generated to protect yourself.

All of this input is then delivered to the "war room" of your brain, where it is analyzed and decisions are made about responses to order the body to make. The analysis step is very complicated and isn't completely understood, but we know that a great deal of it happens using comparisons.

When the information your receptors detect reaches the parts of your brain where a response must be decided, it is compared to stored information: lessons you learned in school, what you've been taught about right and wrong, or memories of previous situations that were like this. Incoming signals are quickly compared to all this stored information. An appropriate response is then determined, and instructions go out to the body to carry it out.

One of the amazing things about this is that these comparisons are made—bouncing around nearly six hundred million interconnecting nerve pathways—while your brain is making thousands of other decisions just to make sure you maintain a normal state of functioning within your body. And the whole sequence happens almost instantaneously.

Neurologic pathways, the constant firing of the receiving-analyzing-responding sequence, are responsible for every response your body makes. This includes the behaviors you don't like.

Let's return to Todd at the mall. The stimulus that entered his eyes was the scantily clad woman. Those erotic images were sent through nerve fibers into his brain. That's step one of the pathway. In the brain, neurons thought about what to do about it. "Well, I could avert my eyes modestly, or I could glue them onto that woman, sucking every ounce of lustful enjoyment out of her. Hmm, tough choice. Eyes, indulge yourselves." That's step two. Step three: the message went back out, and muscles around the eyes and neck gladly obeyed and kept his sight directed toward the object of

HOMEOSTASIS—DEFENDING YOUR STEADY STATE

his pleasure. And with that, the neurologic pathway is complete.

What about Becky? The information that triggered her neurologic pathway was the news that Rick, "the creature," was getting a privilege from their parents. The stimulus was received by the ears and traveled along nerve fibers to the brain where the neurons thought about how to respond. "Rick is evil and must be destroyed. He must be opposed and thwarted at every turn. Mouth, say something nasty." The command goes out to the mouth, and the venomous reply gets voiced.

This is pretty much our lives as humans: receiving, analyzing, and responding to stimuli using neurologic pathways.

The Mind Is a Terrible Thing

In all that discussion of neurons and stimuli, did you catch the fact that thoughts were being formed, memories accessed, and decisions made *by a physical part of your body?* You thought you did all this in your mind, right? Not in some tangled network of organic wiring. People like to think of the human mind as something distinct from the organ called the brain. We like to think of it as independent from our bodies, perhaps residing in a psychological dimension or even in the spirit realm.

But this is simply not so.

Now, don't get me wrong. I don't think anyone claims to fully understand the mind. It is hard to say exactly where we get that internal awareness of self, and if you would like to hold on to the idea that "I think, therefore I am," that's OK with me. But one thing we do know is that your thoughts are clearly centered in the organ called the brain.

In fact, medical research has developed ways to actually see your thoughts happening in your brain. Imaging tools like positron emission tomography (PET) scans, single photon emission computed tomography (SPECT) scans, and functional magnetic resonance imaging (fMRI) allow us to see what portions of the brain are active during different cognitive activities, including thought and learning.

One study with such a device studied patients troubled by obsessive thinking. As cruel as it may sound, these patients were given a stimulus to produce obsessive thoughts, something like: "You left the stove on at home." Then, as they lay there and obsessed, fighting the urge to rush home and check their stove, the technicians did the scan. The portions of the brain responsible for the obsessive thoughts "lit up" on the pictures produced by the scan. The radiologists could literally see the portion of the brain that was thinking obsessively.

So as we'll see throughout this section, the mind is firmly grounded in the physical body—the flesh. That means it is subject to the corruption of sin. And *that* means it is in need of sanctification.

Homeostasis

Why does the body perform these neurologic pathway sequences? And why so many of them? I mean, your body has hundreds of millions of nerve connections that are used in this process. What's the big deal?

The big deal is that your body craves one thing above all else: normalcy.

We all want to be in a nice, quiet, steady state where everything is normal. No hunger. No stress. No hassles. No fights or tension. Not too hot. Not too cold. We just want things to keep going along smoothly. We all are wired that way. The main goal of your brain and all its neurologic pathways is to maintain the status quo. As we have seen, it carefully monitors everything going on inside and out and immediately responds to anything that upsets the body's resting state of normalcy, which is called *homeostasis*.

Now that you know what it means, you can go out and impress your friends by dropping it into conversation: "My, it's getting warm in here. I think I'll take off my jacket to maintain my homeostasis." But it's more than an impressive word. Homeostasis controls your life and you don't even know it. Your body is literally wired to automatically defend against anything that would upset your homeostasis, and your brain works full time to maintain this delicate balance.

Even when you are in a nice, steady state, your brain isn't just sitting and idling. It is carefully monitoring the internal and external environment and making adjustments to respond to

Homeostasis—Defending Your Steady State

alterations. It might be a change in glucose levels or blood concentration that throws off your homeostasis. It could be illness or injury. It could also be a change in emotions, fear, or a perceived threat that makes your body instantly respond to protect its homeostasis. Whatever the problem, your entire physical being is predisposed to pounce on it to make the change go away and return everything to sweet homeostasis.

Are you ready for another five-dollar word? Here it is: neuroendocrine. Your neuroendocrine system is one of the most powerful tools your brain has in its quest to maintain homeostasis. With this your brain (neuro) uses hormones (endocrine) to bring about rapid and powerful responses to things that affect you.

Let's say you're driving along and an oncoming car swerves into your lane. As soon as your eyes see it and deliver the information to the brain, the neuroendocrine system springs into action. The hypothalamus in the brain receives the signal and instantly recognizes it as a danger. It responds by triggering the pituitary and then the adrenal gland. Together these glands produce a wave of hormones—including aldosterone, cortisol, and adrenaline—that flood your system and affect nearly every other organ in the body to get them to respond to the stress. This is referred to as the "fight-or-flight" response. It's the body's way of building up strength to either stand and fight or bolt out of there to avoid danger.

When the fight-or-flight response is activated, the heart pumps faster and stronger because of this rush of hormones. The lungs breathe deeper and more rapidly. Airways open up. The blood vessels tighten to raise blood pressure. Pain sensations are dampened in the brain to maintain clarity of thought. Blood flow is directed away from the intestines to make it available to the vital organs and muscles. Organ function is maintained at these heightened levels until the stress is relieved.

Let's say you swerve off the road and onto the shoulder, and the car passes. You sit there with your heart racing, gasping for air. You may cry uncontrollably, and your hands may shake. Your body then does a quick assessment and realizes that no harm was done and the threat has passed. New signals from neurologic pathways suppress the stress response, and your levels begin to return to normal.

Do you see how one stimulus can affect widespread changes throughout the body, mobilizing the body's energy to defend against whatever has disrupted homeostasis? This can save you from disaster. Used wrongly, it can also bring disaster down upon you.

Defensiveness

This is why a certain word can send a person into a rage, or a quiet fear can set your entire body trembling. Your body is hard-wired to detect problems and counter them almost automatically. Anything that disrupts the flesh's homeostasis is automatically and powerfully resisted.

If the problem the body detects happens to be an infection, this response is very useful at producing healing. If, on the other hand, the disruption happens to be another person upsetting your normalcy, your body's automatic "stress response"—screaming at the person until he leaves you alone, for instance—might not be the best solution to the problem. Reacting in the way that comes naturally (i.e., your fleshly response) may lead to problems in your relationships.

In the mall, Todd wanted to go coasting along looking at the almost nude woman who passed him. That was his homeostasis. But something interrupted that happy state: he was challenged by his wife. Becky wanted to keep slamming her brother, but her mom called her on it. In both cases their desired state of normalcy was challenged, and everything in them mobilized a defense against the threat to their homeostasis in an attempt to get their normalcy back. That's why both situations quickly escalated.

Watch out for defensiveness in your relationships with others. This is the clue that your homeostasis has gotten set on a wrong thing, that your "normal" is being threatened. When you feel yourself reacting defensively, try to take a minute to analyze the situation. What is it that you feel you need to protect? Defensiveness nearly always points to some fleshly response you're trying to coddle.

Which means you are obeying the flesh in that moment. Which means you are sinning.

Homeostasis—Defending Your Steady State

It has been the same ever since Adam and Eve. Whenever we choose to follow the flesh instead of following God's way, it is sin.

> Do you not know that when you present yourselves to someone as slaves for obedience, you are slaves of the one whom you obey, either of sin resulting in death, or of obedience resulting in righteousness?
>
> —Romans 6:16

Our defensiveness in relationships is the normal fleshly response designed to maintain homeostasis. But like Todd's and Becky's flesh, our flesh is corrupted by sin. The very defensive responses that are designed to protect us are now being used to protect wrong behaviors.

So you need to change your homeostasis from maintaining "normal" sinful patterns and get it under God's control to end the problems it causes. You need to reset what is normal on this issue so that the steady state your neuroendocrine system attempts to maintain is one that is consistent with God's will for our behavior. To accomplish that, let's use the treatment plan we described in chapter three and see how we can apply it when fleshly homeostasis mechanisms are controlling you.

The Treatment Plan

Listen

Think about that stubborn problem that's been plaguing you. In the whole sequence of behaviors and choices that surround it, do you ever feel defensive? Does something set you off? Can you feel yourself escalating a situation defensively? If you do, this is a sure sign that the flesh is at work.

Keep in mind that the surface problem that gives you pain is probably not the ultimate problem here. The boss who ticks you off by correcting your work, the spouse who is always nagging, and the friends who always seem to cut you down may not be the problem. Listen, because God may be telling you it is not everyone else that is in need of change.

Also look for those deeper areas making you defensive. Is there some deeper insecurity? Maybe you feel vulnerable because of a hidden weakness, or maybe you're just not used to being attacked. Remember to look for the God issue, too. Are you having trouble believing He'll care for you and defend you? Is there some part of you that feels God has somehow ripped you off, so now you deserve to lash out at others? Keep digging until God shows you the depths of the problem.

Admit

Defensiveness is clearly fleshly. It is your human nature that has you wired to fight off anything or anyone that disrupts your comfortable, steady lifestyle. If you let it control you, it will. Automatically. When you see that happening in any situation—when you feel a defensiveness that seems to arise and take over your mouth and behavior—it is time to admit you have a flesh problem rooted in a wrongly set homeostasis.

You might have trouble accepting that you might be wrong in your belief that it is everyone else who has the problem. Look around your life and see all the relationships that may have been damaged by this sin. Ask God to reveal to you the pain that launching your counterattacks has caused others. The pain you feel in this time of struggling will help convince you of the ugliness of your problem and bring you to a place of real repentance.

When you really believe that the problem is not other people's issues, but *your hair trigger* that is ready to blast people at a moment's notice, you *are* ready to change. Remember, it is not enough to admit that your sharp comebacks are wrong. That's just the surface problem. You have to admit that you are wrong deep inside where your human fleshly nature controls you, making you defend and counterattack rather than deal reasonably with others.

Submit

Submission requires making a critical choice, as we have said. So, how do you make the right choices to submit this problem to God's control if it is all so automatic? It's going to take a work of grace to untangle the neurologic pathways that keep you in bondage to fleshly defensiveness, but it can happen as you begin to submit this area to God.

Here's how it is going to work. You can start by remembering the three distinct steps in the sequence: receiving, analyzing, and responding. Each step has a starting point and an ending point, and it is at those points where you can influence the cycle and interrupt the sin. You can't do a lot about the stimuli that jump in your face. Todd didn't go out looking for a temptress, and Becky certainly wasn't hoping her mom would bring up her brother. The trigger inputs just blindsided them. But you *can* monitor the analysis process and your responses.

When something happens and you feel defensiveness rising up inside you, recognize it as the flesh. The simple act of realizing that this impulse is from the flesh—and is therefore not of God—will give you pause before you react. This may be all you need to give you the opportunity to choose to respond better. But more importantly, that choice of the will is going to open you up to God's grace to come in and start doing some rewiring. And if you blow it this time and only later realize what happened, go back to repentance to continue the work of His grace deep inside. That's what will help you prepare for next time. Yes, have no fear, there will be a next time, since your flesh is still in control. But next time can be different.

Eventually the defensive responses will slow and stop altogether. When Todd's wife asked, "What were you doing?", that would have meant analyzing the situation honestly and recognizing he had a problem. Once acknowledged and repented of, he could have chosen to replace the flesh's automatic responses with, "Oh, wow. I was totally drooling over that chick, wasn't I? Sorry, honey. Maybe we should leave pretty soon." In the same way, had Becky given her defensiveness over to the Lord during her conversation with her mom, she could have chosen to hold her tongue rather than giving her defensiveness free rein.

You can do this, too. It is God's will that areas now surrendered to the flesh be brought under submission to Him.

Trust

It's not that easy, you say? No, it certainly isn't—especially if you've reacted like this so often it's become a strong fleshly bondage for you. But as God does a work of grace inside you, you will find that this little pause will grow and you'll have more time to consider your responses.

I think you can see now why trying real hard in your own strength to defeat this sin is useless. The neurologic pathways that provide homeostasis are some of the most encompassing and deeply rooted. You can never change them on your own. Your body's systems are mobilized against a change to what they consider the status quo. You're going to have to trust God to do it. Remind yourself that God not only promised to forgive you of sin, but He also promised to cleanse you of it. Make that your prayer now and trust in that promise.

Stand firm

If you find that defensiveness is your main area of sin, and you're having trouble defeating it, don't give up the fight. You know what's at work now. And remember, the problem lies deep in your inner desires for the flesh. Just hang on as God does a thorough work of sanctification to rid you of this problem once and for all.

Continue to evaluate the things that set off your anger, frustration, or other defense mechanisms. Do similar situations or the same types of people set you off? Maybe there is something deeper that God is trying to say you need to deal with. Keep listening.

Maybe somewhere deep inside, you actually *like* the defensive responses you give because they make you feel powerful or in control. It's going to be tough to really admit this is wrong and submit it to God if deep down inside you like it. Ask God to bring you to the point where you can give this up. But hold on tight! You're probably headed for another lap through the wilderness.

As you're standing firm on this issue, fill your life with God's Word, prayer, and worship to strengthen your spirit in dealing with the flesh. And get out there and get some fellowship. You can get a good relationship workout by interacting with other Christians who will love and support you as you deal with your issue.

CHAPTER 5

DRIVES—FLESHLY DRIVENNESS

IN this chapter we'll be meeting Jeff and Cynthia. (Todd and Becky have the day off.)

JEFF

Jeff loves online computer games. Not those "twitch games" that kids play on X-Box, but a specialized kind of Internet game called a MMORPG, Massively Multiplayer Online Role-Playing Game.

In this game, which we'll call *Shadowblade,* Jeff has created an awesome character: a 26th-level human Ranger with night vision and a +5 Bow of Smiting. In the *Shadowblade* world, Jeff is a man of stature. He is a high-ranking member of a Ranger's guild, and he is thinking of splitting off to form a new guild, knowing that up to fifty of his online comrades-in-arms would go with him.

Every weeknight until two or three in the morning and all day and night every weekend (except for church on Sundays), Jeff is at the computer. Empty Mountain Dew cans and frozen food cartons surround his monitor, along with stacks of unopened mail.

Jeff is a bachelor, so no one really minds that he spends his time this way. Except that lately his hunger to be playing the game has been growing much stronger. It doesn't help that at his job he's at the bottom of the food chain. And since he works at a fast-food joint, he's at the bottom of a food chain's food chain.

A couple of weeks ago the manager hired a new kid who's a real go-getter. The kid's crazy to fry potatoes. And he wants more and more hours. Maybe it's all in Jeff's head, but he's getting the feeling that the manager would like it if he just quit so he could give all his hours to the new kid.

He hates his job. Nobody likes him there. Yesterday a baby threw up on the play equipment. Guess who had to climb in the ball pool and clean it all up? Not Golden Boy, that's for sure.

If Jeff could figure out how to do it and survive, he *would* quit the job, gladly, and spend all his time playing online. But the only thing that's keeping him in Mountain Dew and frozen burritos—not to mention paying his monthly Internet and game fees—is this crummy job.

Shadowblade, take me away!

Cynthia

Cynthia isn't getting any younger. All of her friends are already married by now—or at least engaged or seriously committed. But who is coming around asking her out? Nobody. What's the matter with her anyway? She's not overweight or leprous or anything. She has a lot to offer, if a boy would just take the time to notice.

She's been praying quite a bit lately. "God, are You up there? Can't You see I'm lonely here? Are You hiding Mr. Right in another dimension or something? Tell You what, I'd settle for Mr. OK if You'd just bring him on by."

Over time, Cynthia's wardrobe gradually changes. The prim and proper "nice girl" clothes have gradually been replaced with a new look. If her mother saw her now, she would freak: pierced eyebrow, revealing blouse with only one strap, open midriff, heavy makeup, and jeans so tight she needs a shoehorn to get them on. And guess what? Now she's getting lots of attention from boys. Everywhere she goes she has them flocking after her. What a great feeling to replace the loneliness.

But why are the guys such losers? Seems like they're all after only one thing. Oh, well, beggars can't be choosers.

You Drive Me Crazy

Do you know anyone like Jeff and Cynthia? Are *you* anything like either one?

You may not see a common denominator between them, so I'll give it away early: they are both committing unwise, even sinful, behaviors because of a basic fleshly need they're driven to meet. For Jeff, it's a feeling of worth. In *Shadowblade*, he's an important guy, respected and powerful. In his real life he's low on the totem pole and merely tolerated by those around him. In the game he's rich and popular. In reality, he's poor and lonely. Of course, he doesn't see that he could achieve good things in the real world if he just devoted as much attention to it as he does to the game. All he knows is that there, in *Shadowblade*, he feels better than he feels anywhere else.

Cynthia's not sure what's going on with herself. If she could see deep down, she'd see that she wants male affection and is afraid of being alone in her life. She wants to be held by strong arms and told that she's safe and cherished. But all she can see is that for some reason she likes her new clothes—even though they're much different from her image as a good Christian girl—and that every Friday night she finds herself walking the mall, dressed like a sleaze, hoping for something good to happen.

There's nothing wrong with Jeff's and Cynthia's inner desires, even if they could know them. Wanting to be loved or to feel worthwhile are good desires, given by God. The problem comes when those desires run out of control and begin to lead us into sin. And that situation—normal drives set at non-normal levels—is what we're talking about in this chapter.

Animal Attraction

We like to think we're above animals when it comes to instincts. "No, we don't have animal instincts. We don't fly south for the winter, and we certainly aren't controlled by anything so base as animal urges."

The truth is, we do have these instincts. Humans have instincts every bit as much as animals do. We just call them by another name. We say we have *drives*, not instincts. Animals have a mating instinct. We have a sex drive. Geese fly south for the winter. We summer in Florida. Big difference. Call it what you will, you and I are driven to perform many of our behaviors because of this very basic human function.

What do you think is the strongest human drive? If you were thinking the sex drive, you're not even close. The drive for sex is strong, to be sure—strong enough to create families that last; strong enough to bring down relationships, careers, even leaders of nations. But there are stronger drives. Like to try another guess? How about the drive to succeed? Still not it.

The strongest human drive is much simpler. It is the drive to breathe. Surprised? Well, consider how long you would be able to live without satisfying one of the lesser drives, such as success, before making a change in your life. Some people work years without success before making a move. How long would you tolerate not having sex before you decided to pursue it? But how long would you tolerate not breathing before you decided to do something about it? Get the point? You will not allow anything to cover your mouth and nose for more than a few *seconds* before you instinctually respond.

I don't care how passive a person you are, how much you prefer nonviolent resolutions to situations, or even how spiritual you are, if someone blocks your airway for more than just a few seconds, you will take aggressive action. You will kick, punch, and bite the person if necessary to fulfill your drive to breathe. If you happen to have a knife or gun handy, you might instinctively use it against your attacker regardless of your feelings about violence. The drive to breathe is just too strong. In the appropriate circumstances, it will control your behavior.

Would you like to guess what the second strongest drive is? Maybe now you are catching on. After breathing, the next most powerful drive is the drive to drink (water, that is). After that come the drives to eat, sleep, and reproduce, roughly in descending order. And there are others. Drives are programmed into your flesh so that you will have some basic guidelines in order to stay healthy and reproduce yourself, much in the same way animals do. These instincts—I mean, *drives*—are given to us to ensure that our needs are met for survival.

Drives—Fleshly Drivenness

These drives affect us subconsciously. That's why they're so difficult to identify. But if we could see them all, we would find that they influence many, if not most, of our behaviors.

For example, many of our responses in relationships arise from a *drive* to be loved. The job we do, the clothes we wear, and the car we own may all have been chosen to fulfill a drive for self-esteem, which includes having the respect of others and feeling useful. Our drive to protect ourselves can be detected when we react to any attack, real or perceived, physical or emotional. Even the pursuit of sex comes from a drive—instinctual reproductive behavior, perhaps, but in men, more likely from yet another drive: the drive for pleasure.

One of our stronger instincts seems to be the drive to control the environment around us. This drive is probably behind new methods for farming and tracking the weather. It may also affect us more personally, however, as it leads us to want to control other people around us. This drive has likely lead to numerous fights among family members and possibly even wars between countries.

Your Internal Thermostat

Where do drives come from? Some abstract thought process in your mind? No. Just as with animal instincts, human drives are firmly rooted in the physical.

Our drives stem from many of the same mechanisms that maintain homeostasis. They are primarily controlled in an area of the brain known as the *hypothalamus*. The hypothalamus monitors all of our bodily functions to help maintain a normal state of function. The hypothalamus works something like the thermostat in your home. It sets a high and low setting for all the things you need to live. The "sweet spot" between the two extremes is what your brain considers normal.

Just like in your house, when your body temperature drops too low, the hypothalamus kicks on the body's furnace and raises your temperature. If it needs to drive up your blood pressure, the hypothalamus turns up the heart rate and tightens the blood vessels until the upper level is reached and the "drive" to raise the blood stops.

You may never consciously notice most of these drives. They go on inside your body all the time, quietly maintaining homeostasis. But some drives affect you consciously. If you're in a smoky room and your hypothalamus notes that you're not getting enough oxygen, it will trigger a change in your breathing. If that does not satisfy your neurologic drive to maintain proper oxygen levels, you will be "driven" to seek out cleaner air. This may require moving your body outside. This is an example of your body's drives affecting your behavior in a conscious way.

Inner drives affect not only our behavior but also other people. A hungry baby is a good example. The baby's inner drives cause kicking, screaming, and crying to affect those around him until he gets what he needs. Do you ever find yourself kicking, screaming, and crying to get what you want? It's the same inner drives at work.

These drives can be quite strong. I hope you never learn just how strong the drive to drink can be by getting caught in the desert without water. How about being caught in a traffic jam with no bathroom? Pretty strong drive, huh? As the need goes unmet, the drive grows stronger and stronger until it consumes you. Your thoughts and actions begin to revolve around the problem until the need is met.

So far we've been talking about physical needs: breathing, drinking, relieving the bladder. But the hypothalamus regulates other kinds of needs, drives, and levels, too. Just as a fall in glucose produces a signal that is sent to the liver to convert glycogen into glucose to produce fast energy, a fall in sexual activity would send signals that produce behaviors that attract more sexual activity.

The terrorist attacks on the World Trade Center in New York City and the Pentagon in Washington DC sent people flocking to church. Why? These attacks set off warning lights in millions of people: "Danger, danger! Sense of security levels dropping radically. Increase feelings of security immediately!" And so they crammed the pews. When people felt safe again, the warning lights went off, and church attendance dropped to its pre-9/11 level.

Many of our responses are just this basic. We may think we are sincerely and carefully considering our responses, when actually our hypothalamus is just driving us in one direction or another.

It's the flesh at work. And you thought you were so in control, didn't you? You thought you were far above being driven about by animal instincts, huh? Oh, well.

Let's look back to our hapless examples from above. Do you think "Jedi Jeff" ever sat down and said, "I'm going to go play video games to increase my sense of self-worth"? How about "Sleazy Cindy"? Did she go shopping one day to pick out revealing clothes to attract guys to make her feel loved? Of course not. They were driven to these behaviors by deep, subconscious brain centers inside their flesh.

NEVER ENOUGH

So what? They got their needs met, right? That's the point, isn't it? Well, yes and no. The flesh does help us get our needs met—and that's good. But we will never get our needs fully met (at least not without a lot of other problems) by fleshly drivenness—and that's bad. These fleshly functions are not wrong by themselves. It's not wrong to desire respect or affection. God designed these drives as a way for us to acquire the things we need.

The problem is that the "normal" settings in the hypothalamus have been corrupted by sin. In some cases the low point has been set at artificially high levels, telling you that you need more of these things—pleasure, respect, affection, etc.—than you really do. In other cases the high point has been reset, letting you tolerate more and more of things like violence, hatred, and resentment before signaling a problem. Your strong inner drives are now controlled by sin, so they pressure you toward sinful behaviors.

The flesh, which once was programmed to want just enough money to provide for your family, now demands enough money to buy lots of "stuff" and influence people—it wants bags of money! Your settings for sexual activity used to be set at a level that would provide for a loving and lasting marriage. But this is no longer enough. The flesh pushes you to want it more frequently and with more excitement—until the fleshly pressure cannot be fulfilled by one person and you are "driven" out into the world to find more.

The end of fleshly drivenness is not satisfaction, as we tend to believe, but *despair*. Why? Because the levels for fleshly pleasures are set too high. The needs never really get met, at least for long, or they are met in excessive and damaging ways.

Changing the settings on your fleshly thermostats is the key to seeing change in the area of drivenness. In the winter, I turn the thermostat down to save money. The family gets cold and turns it back up. I find it up and turn it down. They get cold and turn it up. Sound familiar? The same battle goes on in your life. Defeating fleshly drivenness comes down to one thing: control of the thermostat. Who gets to set the levels in the hypothalamus?

This can be a difficult battle, primarily because your hypothalamus is a subconscious brain center. You can't change it willfully as you can the thermostat in your home. But the truth remains: if you want to stop being driven to sin by your out-of-whack drives, the "levels" have to be reset to the settings God intended.

Across the Line

To protect its flow of pleasurable sensations, the flesh can urge a person to do horrifying things. An addict who is suddenly unable to afford his drug may become a thief, mugger, or even a murderer. In the same way, we can become addicted to praise or adrenaline or attraction from the opposite sex. And if our supply of the good stuff is threatened, we are capable of things we'd never imagine.

The principle is this: when a person's flesh becomes accustomed to receiving good feelings through something, and that something is taken away or threatened, he becomes capable of all manner of atrocity.

A woman feels loved when she is around a man that is not her husband. He gives her things her husband can't or won't. She wants to run away with him—but there's the problem of her children. He doesn't want children and keeps pointing to that whenever she talks about running off. Two weeks later she calls 911 because her children have accidentally drowned.

A man is in the right place at the right time to play an instrumental role in rescuing a child. He receives a barrage of media attention. His face is everywhere in the news. But then the world begins to move on to other interests. Soon afterward he recaptures the media attention by saving a child from a burning building—but is then arrested for starting the fire himself. To get the rush back, he crossed his own boundaries of acceptable behavior.

A life ruled by the flesh is a terrifying thing. Good citizens have been turned into traitorous spies. Husbands have murdered their wives. Firefighters have started forest fires. Athletes have taken performance-enhancing drugs. Smart students have cheated on tests.

If you find yourself breaking rules you've always upheld, if you look at yourself and say, "What are you *doing?*", consider that your flesh may be ruling you, and seek help from the treatment plan.

Treatment Plan

Listen

The best place to start in your informed listening phase is to identify the ways you are driven to your recurring sin. Look for the things that lead to a sense of inner pressure compelling you to act: "I *have* to go to the dance—all my friends will be there," or "I don't care if it uproots my family; I *need* a better paying job." This pressure may be a sign of the flesh driving you.

Be alert too when you feel you have to pressure someone else to get something you need or want. "I know you want to wait until marriage, but if you love me, you'll show me now." That's the flesh at work. In marriage it could show up as pressuring your spouse toward doing something you would find fulfilling or enjoyable but which he or she would not. Even if you feel your spouse is unnecessarily uptight in this area, when the Spirit is in control, you will wait until the other person is ready.

If you sense this pressure in you, you've identified that the flesh is at work. Try to spot the need you are pressured to fulfill (or are pressuring someone else to fulfill), and you will have gone a long way toward conquering it. Sometimes just recognizing the problem will be enough to end it in your life. Take Cynthia, for example. If she could just realize that she was pressured to dress flirtatiously in order to attract men, she might stop and say, "What a fool I'm being. These clothes are gone. I'm dressing modestly from now on."

Where could your God issue be in this one? You'll have to wrestle with God to figure it out for your particular circumstance, but drives are about getting your needs met. Do you feel God isn't giving you something you need? Feeling a little ripped off? Keep listening: you're getting to the bottom.

`Admit`

Drivenness is as fleshly a response as any you will encounter. It is programmed into you deeply, as deeply as the instinct that makes rams bang their heads into things. So if you feel like you're banging your head against a wall at times, it just might be because you're controlled by fleshly drives.

The problem with drives is that they are so deeply imprinted on your nature that it may be tough to understand why you're doing what you're doing. Stuff just kind of happens. Since these behaviors feel so natural, it might be hard to see them as wrong. You might even find yourself defending your wrong actions: "That's just the way I am."

In fact, that *is* just the way you are. You are fleshly. But that doesn't mean you get to keep acting like that, not if you're a Christian. The Holy Spirit, who is alive within you, is going to go to work to change you. Where He meets resistance He'll turn up the pressure and allow some struggling to get your attention. People are going to respond negatively to you pressuring them. When people around you feel pushed, they'll push back, and you'll be butting heads with people. When this happens and you're the one putting the screws to everyone else because of the way your flesh is pressuring you, admit it as sin and get it dealt with.

You might also find that people close to you sense you are pressured in some direction, and they are grabbing hold of you trying to drag you back. You might see it as your wife standing in the way of you going out and buying that third set of golf clubs after Jerry Jones down at the club got his. But really she is just sensing your fleshly drivenness to keep up with the Joneses, and she's trying to help. Or maybe your brother keeps hassling you when you're going out to the casino again. Don't write off these people as being unsupportive or party poopers until you've examined your flesh in this area.

Submit

When Cynthia recognized her flesh was pressuring her to put out the vibe in inappropriate ways, she moved pretty easily through the admission and submission stages. She let the lid off the pressure cooker, and her problem disappeared fairly quickly, as often happens when your eyes are really opened to a problem.

Jeff might have a little more of a problem. He really likes his diversion and will probably hold on to it harder. It will be that much tougher to make those important choices that turn away from the flesh and toward the Spirit. It is also meeting very essential needs of self-esteem and autonomy. In these situations God is going to bring Jeff into a time of struggling to break his enjoyment of this fleshly diversion. The harder he holds on to the fleshly behavior, the harder God is going to press His finger on him. It might take him losing his job and having his computer repossessed, or something worse. God will do what it takes.

God loves us enough to take away the thing that's holding us back, even if we've come to cherish it. He wants your internal settings to align with what He's set out in the system guidelines. If you are His child, He will not allow you to continue operating at the wrong drive levels. He will oppose you until He gets your attention.

As the flesh puts on the pressure, God turns up the pressure as well to bring you to the place where you are willing to submit your problem to His control and start making some good choices. That's a lot of pressure, and that's what struggling under God's sanctifying Spirit is all about. Eventually you will hopefully get tired of the stress and give it over to God.

This is a tough one. Breaking the power of deeply rooted drives often takes pulling out Watchman Nee's prayer of *committing to God that which you cannot submit*. It may also take a few laps through the wilderness before the flesh gives up.

Trust

More than ever you are going to have to trust God to do a work deep inside you. Ask Him to adjust the knobs to the correct settings on your inner thermostats. Pray that He dials down your desires for lust, power, greed, or whatever is out of proportion to God's plan.

Don't bother trying to change your own settings. You can't reach in and adjust your own hypothalamus or any of your other fleshly control centers. But God can, and struggling is one of the ways He does it. As you try to get your needs met with fleshly mechanisms and fail over and over, you eventually start to get the message. You don't have to hit yourself on the head with a brick many times before the pain teaches you it is a dumb thing to do.

To participate in the work God is doing, you can immerse yourself in His Word. There you will find what needs He intended mankind to have and how to fulfill them. Learning His Word will help build your faith in God's way of doing things. As you begin to trust in His way to get your needs met, the flesh loses power and the Spirit takes control.

Stand firm

Beating your inherent drives requires standing firm on the biblical truths about how God wants things done. You may have been raised to believe that getting your sexual needs met requires playing the field and test-driving a number of models before settling down on your final selection. You're going to have to stand firm on the knowledge that God has a better plan for relationships than that.

You might be naturally driven to succeed. Maybe the stress you're getting at home is the struggling God is sending to let you know you have to turn it down a notch and start being home more. As you choose to commit less time to work and more to your home and church, you may see a few clients slip away and a few dollars pass you by. That will be the time to stand firm and know you are storing up far greater treasures in heaven. As your sense of struggle fades away and you see positive change taking place in your life, you will know you're getting some of your heavenly treasure paid in advance.

CHAPTER 6

REFLEXES—CONDITIONED RESPONSES

JOANNE

"Mom! Would you please stop moving my stuff!"

Every time Joanne visits her son's dorm room, he complains about something. He claims she's always rearranging furniture and snooping in his underwear drawer. Of course, it's not true. Well, maybe it's a little true. But what's a mother for if not to tidy up her son's room when she can? He says it embarrasses him and makes him feel like a child all over again. How silly. He's twenty years old.

Still, on those rare occasions when Joanne stops to think about it, she does find it odd that she kind of just drops back into Supermom mode whenever she's around him. She finds herself picking up after him without thinking, like she's on autopilot. Usually she just shrugs, reasoning that some habits die hard.

"Oh, look, son, your shoe's untied. Let me—"

"*Mom!*"

STEVE

"Steve? This is David Wills from the church."

"Oh, hi."

"Sorry to call you at home. Do you have a minute?"

Steve mutes the TV, feeling a strange heaviness descend upon him. "I guess."

"Great, thanks. Well, as you probably know, I'm in charge of vacation Bible school at the church this year."

Here it comes, Steve thinks, feeling the weight pressing him into the couch. "Hmm."

"I was meeting with my directors last night, and Debbie Olson said that you and she used to go to the same church where you directed a Sunday school department. Is that right?"

"Yeah. That's right." *Thanks a lot, Debbie.*

"She says you're really great with the kids. Steve, I still need quite a few teachers and directors for VBS. Would you consider serving in that capacity?"

"Yeah, sure."

"Uh...oh, that's great. Would you like to hear more about what we're thinking of doing?"

"No, that's OK. I'm kinda busy right now, but I'll get up to speed at your teachers' meetings. When's the next one?"

"We're going to meet every Thursday evening until the program starts in three months."

"That's fine. I'll be there."

Steve puts the phone down and turns the TV sound up again.

That's just great. There go my Thursday nights. Why did I say yes?

Pavlov's Humans

At the end of the nineteenth century, Ivan Petrovich Pavlov studied reflex behavior in dogs. His most famous experiments went something like this: Every time his lab dogs were about to be given their meal, he would ring a bell. After repeating this process many times, he found that he could cause the dogs to salivate even without food—simply by ringing the bell.

The dogs had come to associate the bell with food. Normally, a dog wouldn't think anything of a bell ringing. But by making the bell/food connection so many times, the dogs' bodies began to respond to the sound of the bell without any processing having to go on in their brains.

Humans are the same way. After we've done something over and over, it becomes almost automatic for us. We don't even have to think about it.

Take typing, for instance. Hunt-and-peck typists spend a lot of time and mental energy searching out the correct letters on the keyboard, while the fingers of skilled typists fly across the keys almost on their own, independent of conscious thought. Just as with Pavlov's dogs, the typist's body responds to the input automatically, without ever troubling the conscious mind for instructions for what to do about it.

Switching to Automatic

How does this happen? In a word, *reflexes*.

You've probably had your reflexes tested by a doctor tapping on your knee and making your leg jump. He was testing your knee-jerk reflex. Reflexes are actually specialized nerve pathways that are designed to give quick, consistent responses in certain situations. The knee-jerk reflex, for example, is designed to give a rapid response to the patellar tendon (attached to your kneecap) getting stretched. The reflex causes the leg to move so it can avoid injury.

Remember the neurologic pathways from chapter four: sensing, analyzing, responding? Well, reflexes are neurologic pathways, too. But what's unique about them is that there is no *analysis* step between step one, receiving a stimulus, and step three, responding. The input fibers for reflexes travel to the spinal cord where they have been hard-wired directly to the muscle response fibers, so a response is made without the involvement of the brain.

Since the brain is not involved, no decision can be made, and the same response is automatically given every time. In the case of the knee-jerk reflex, the same leg movement is produced every time the sensory signal comes from the knee. Though this limits the variety of responses you can give, the payoff is that it speeds up the response tremendously.

True reflexes are "wired in" to you from birth. There's nothing you can do about them—nor would you want to. But God has given the brain an amazing capability to do some rewiring of its own, creating something very similar to reflexes in order to cut down on how long it takes to get from the input to the response.

Our typing example is a good illustration of this. We're not hard-wired to type. It is a skill that has to be learned. But virtually anyone can learn to do it. And the better you get at typing, the less time your brain spends thinking where that pesky "z" key is, until it spends no time thinking about it at all. When you start to spell "zoo," the left pinkie goes to the key without hesitation and, more importantly, without thought. It's as if the knowledge of where the keys are has been transferred directly to the fingers themselves without having to involve the brain.

That's an oversimplification, of course, but it demonstrates the principle: the brain likes to automate things. When it can do so, responses fire off much more quickly, and the brain is freed up to concentrate on the truly important issues, such as what to have for lunch. The brain is always on the lookout for situations in which you're repeatedly responding to something in the same way. The more you respond this way, the more you reinforce the connection, until the brain just decides that everyone would be better served by this being a more or less direct connection. The result is a nerve pathway that looks very similar to a reflex because the analysis step is shortened or cut out altogether.

This amazing ability the brain has to adapt and change these responses is called *plasticity*. This is what allows your brain to develop neurologic pathways on the fly as it needs to in order to deal with the varying sensory inputs it encounters. When your brain notices that you are dealing with a particular input nerve pathway over and over and producing similar responses every time, like always unbuckling and getting out of your car the same way, it simply connects the two.

Here's an example of how out of the loop your brain can be: One day I asked my transcriptionist to proofread my letters for grammatical mistakes as she typed. She surprised me when she said that she'd be happy to proofread, but that she would have to go back and do it after she had typed the letters. Why? Because while she is typing, she has little or no idea what is actually being said in the letters she is transcribing.

And now you know how this happens. The words bypass the reading centers in the brain and go straight to the muscular centers that control her fingers. In that moment, the words are not really words at all; they are only auditory stimuli passing through her brain via high-speed reflex-like nerve pathways directly to her fingers.

Reflexes—Conditioned Responses

Practice Makes Perfect

These automated responses are what allow us to produce what we would commonly call habits. Too often our habits become *bad* habits, so you may see automated responses as a bad thing. But there are some very important benefits to this fleshly aspect of your body that make it part of the good thing that God designed for you.

Whenever you practice some task—whether it is striking keys on a keyboard, kicking a soccer ball into a goal, strumming the strings of a guitar, or doing the box step—what you are really doing is developing reflex-like neurologic pathways. You are conditioning your brain so that you no longer have to think about what you're doing. Your actions become automatic. This allows you to improve the speed and efficiency of your actions.

Just imagine me, who hasn't played much baseball since Little League, standing in front of a major league professional pitcher trying to hit his fastball. I would watch the pitcher go through his windup and release the ball. Then my eyes would begin tracking the ball, and my mind would attempt to estimate its speed, trajectory, time to arrival, and its location when it crosses the plate so that I could determine where to swing the bat to hit the ball.

Probably you can guess what would happen. As the ball whizzed past at nearly one hundred miles per hour I would stand there stunned, without even moving. My arms would never even get a response signal because my brain was bogged down in the analysis step.

Now put a major league batter in the batter's box, and the result is different. Why? Thousands of hours in the batting cage swinging at millions of pitches has developed in him reflex-like, lightning-fast nerve pathways that connect what he is seeing with his eyes directly to his arms—without accessing his brain's analysis centers. The visual input causes a nearly instantaneous response in the muscles of the arms to adjust the bat very quickly, and he hits the ball.

Stress Relief

But it's not all about fastballs, and it's not all about speed. Reflex responses also reduce the stress of living. If you had to go through every day making every little decision as if it were the first time you ever considered it, you would be overwhelmed before leaving the house. Which arm do I use to turn off the alarm? Which leg should I swing out of bed first? Should I take a shower next or eat breakfast? Right sock first or left? Right shoe first or left? As you can see, it could be quite a dilemma.

When our responses involve behaviors that are more complex than just hitting a ball, we tend to refer to these repetitive behaviors as *conditioned responses* or, more commonly, *habits*. But they are really still just neurologic pathways that the body is creating to respond like reflexes. Developing these conditioned responses helps us avoid stress by keeping us from having to deal with difficult situations more than just a few times.

I think back to elementary school when we had assigned seats. I remember wishing we could pick our own seats like the big kids in junior high. I imagined sitting in a different seat every day, just because I could. The funny thing, though, was that when junior high came, we all sat in different seats for the first few days, but we quickly settled into a spot where we stayed for the rest of the semester. Our brains just didn't want to face the stress of making that decision every day. There were too many more important things to focus on in junior high—like the girl sitting two rows up (but that's a different chapter on the flesh).

It may have been a long time since junior high for you, but the same is still true. You just have too many things to focus your attention on throughout the day, so your brain is learning through practice to produce conditioned responses to situations that you deal with repeatedly. In this way your life is made just a little easier.

So I put my left sock on before my right. It's all good, right? Well, not always.

When the reflex-like behavior leads to a good thing—a higher batting average or a quicker morning routine, for instance—we have no reason to think about how we arrived at it. But it is also possible for us to generate reflex-like behaviors that lead to a bad thing, like impulse eating or hitting loved ones. Or what if the stimulus that we're no longer sending to our analysis centers, and therefore not really listening to or thinking about, is our spouse or children?

This is one way we can commit habitual sin without even thinking much about it. And this is when we need to start thinking about dealing with our fleshly conditioned responses.

Emotional Reflexes

Here's another problem you might not have considered: it is not only physical actions that become reflex-like behaviors. We can develop conditioned responses around anything that travels to our brain through the nervous system. Even those inputs that come from deeper sensations, such as our emotions, can be turned into automated responses.

What if I were to tell you that today I saw a kitten get hit by a car? You would probably say, "Oh, that's so sad!" Do you see that you had an almost instantaneous *emotional* response—a knee-jerk reaction, if you will. We are all conditioned to see defenseless, little kittens being killed as a bad thing. If you were a mouse, however, you might not feel as bad. Your reflex-like responses would generate a different emotion.

Now think of your father. Just the mention of his name probably causes some well-programmed feelings to surface. Those feelings may be good or bad, but the point is that they surface quickly because of these fast, reflex-like pathways that have been established over years of dealing with him. This is true for any of the people close to you, because you have had a long time to receive stimuli from them, and it is repeated stimuli that develop reflex responses.

If the stimulus you receive is especially strong, it will help these reflex pathways to develop a stronger reflex response. Child abuse, repetitive ridicule, or recurring failures, for example, produce very strong and very fast reflex responses. In the same way, highly positive stimuli can give strong, fast reflex responses. Reminders of a loved one, vacations, or Christmas, for instance, can quickly generate a positive conditioned emotional response.

These reflex-like responses have a profound affect on relationships. You are responding to those around you based on past conditioning. Your brain deals with the people you interact with regularly just as it deals with how you put your socks on every day. It doesn't want to decide over and over how to respond to everyone you come across. It wants to accomplish the most common interactions automatically and save time and energy for new or unique situations.

When things are good, this can be good. But when things are bad—like when sin is present in us messing things up—this can be bad. For most of us, this is very often bad. Which means we have to get on with a treatment plan for our reflex-like behaviors.

Treatment Plan

Listen

When it comes to dealing with situations and people, this tendency to automate your responses happens very naturally, so it may be tough to spot. You may have dealt disrespectfully with your boss so many times that now it has become a reflex. Now it affects the tone of nearly every response you make to him. You do it without thinking.

Do you always respond to frustration with anger? Have past disappointments led to a conditioned response in which you are always expecting failure? Maybe a series of hurts has led you to knee-jerk attacks against anyone who offers even the slightest criticism. Do the same hurtful words blurt out whenever you find yourself in a certain kind of situation? Do painful emotions surge at the mere mention of a person's name? Maybe you find yourself responding with sarcasm way too often.

It could even be good things. Are you away fixing leaky sinks for everyone else in the neighborhood and then arguing with your wife because you haven't fixed hers? Maybe you reach for your wallet to give a quick gift to mend hurts with your children, but you find your relationships are still sinking. You may need to examine some of these behaviors as possible sources of your problems. Ask God to show you.

If you are reacting wrongly because of this "evil autopilot," you are being controlled by the flesh in your reflex responses. You have developed sinful conditioned responses. If the flesh is controlling you at any point, it will lead to problems. In times of struggling, look for these repetitive responses, even repetitive feelings, to help you spot this area of the flesh at work in your life.

Think back to Joanne. She's been mothering her son for nearly twenty years. That's plenty of time to develop ingrained conditioned responses in her interactions with him. Unfortunately, things are changing in their relationship. He is becoming a mature and independent man. Her automatic responses toward him need to change. However, if her reflex-like responses toward her son are controlled by her flesh, there will be a problem. These behaviors are programmed and don't change easily—in fact, homeostasis causes them to *resist* change—so as their relationship changes, there will be a rub with these old behaviors.

Conditioned responses, since they occur as quick decisions in a situation, may look like impulsiveness, too. Do you impulsively buy things when you experience something that makes you feel bad about yourself? Do you head for the fridge whenever you are bored or hurt or lonely? *Aha!* You have begun to identify an area where your flesh may be controlling you with conditioned responses.

Here's another good example of the flesh at work: you can use these conditioned nerve pathways to allow words to go from a hymnal, song sheet, or screen through your eyes and directly out your mouth during worship. This leaves your mind free to think about how much you have to do to get ready for work tomorrow, how mad you are at the kids for making your late for church (again), and how silly Mrs. Edwards looks in that hat three pews up. Think about this the next time you're at church, and you may catch yourself doing it.

Did you ever wonder what Jesus meant when He talked about worshiping in spirit and in truth? Well, one thing I know is that if you're worshiping using fleshly reflexes, that probably isn't what He had in mind.

When God brings your mind to the spot where your knee-jerk reactions come out, you've found the place to start dealing with this area of the flesh. And if you are relying on your flesh's quick comebacks rather than waiting for God's input, it might be because you really don't think much of the input God is going to give in your life. Do a little digging in this area, and you might unearth a hidden God issue.

Admit

I think you can see how conditioned responses arise from the plasticity of your neurologic processes, showing them as flesh, plain and simple. Healing begins when you admit where this area of flesh is controlling you and leading to problems.

Remember that more insidious way your flesh can control you even when you are doing good things? Even where your fleshly mechanisms produce what are normally thought of as good behaviors, if the flesh is in control, *it is wrong and will lead to problems* because "those who are in the flesh cannot please God" (Romans 8:8). Now it is time for those advanced levels of repentance we talked about in chapter three. You cannot fully repent of your fleshly sin until you admit this aspect as well.

Let's look at Steve's responses to Will from church. It is a pretty common interchange between Christians, one you may have had yourself. There is a need at church in ministry. Steve has been active before, so Will calls him to fill the slot. Steve's response—"Sure, why not?"—comes almost without thinking. Why? Because it's the answer he always gives. It is a conditioned response. He doesn't even think about it anymore. Well, volunteering for ministry is a good thing, isn't it? But in this case, Steve is not responding to the call of the Spirit. He doesn't even want to do it, but he says *yes* anyway. It's the call of the flesh that motivates him now.

You've likely been in this situation before and know what happens. You grudgingly accept a responsibility at church. You do your best to be happy and excited about the task because you want to be a good Christian and serve God. Filling the role, however, is a burden that becomes increasingly difficult to carry. Your frustration grows until eventually you lash out at someone you are working with, and feelings are hurt.

When the load becomes too great, you start pulling back, dropping responsibilities, and you begin to suffer the accusations (from yourself and the growing list of people you're hurting in the process) of not being a committed Christian or of letting your brothers and sisters down. Finally, you stop ministry altogether and decide you are burned out. In the end you wonder why God let you down and didn't supply the strength you needed for ministry. You stepped up and made a commitment, but God didn't hold up His end of the bargain. You are left confused and struggling.

The problem is not with God, my friend; it is with you. There was no spiritual power to fulfill your commitment because you were not functioning in the power of the Spirit. Your flesh controlled the process from the beginning. Even though the external behavior looked good, the flesh was in control—which made the outcome bad.

No matter how good a response may look, if a conditioned response is generating your behavior, *it is the flesh that is in control*. If the flesh is in control, it will always lead to sin in your life. That's all the flesh knows how to do. If you let it drive, it will eventually crash. Every time.

Keep an ear out for this as you are listening to God telling you where the flesh is active in your life, and then lump it in with all the bad stuff you are repenting of also, and you'll be on your way to victory.

```
Submit
```

If you have developed patterns of reflex-like responses that are controlled by the flesh, you need to have those reflexes broken up. Somehow the analysis step in the neurologic pathway process has to be reinserted.

Remember that term *plasticity*? It created this problem in the first place by allowing those repetitive responses to turn into reflex-like behaviors to save time and energy. The great news about plasticity is that it works both ways. If you notice conditioned behaviors that aren't working the way you want anymore, those connections can be rewired.

Right now you may have a direct link between stimulus and response. If it's leading you to sin, that wire needs to be snipped. Once cut, you can reinsert the analysis portion of the neurologic pathway formation process, and you can determine new responses that are better.

Trying to muster up enough willpower on your own to

change these behaviors is not going to help. The analysis step is being bypassed, remember? So making that critical choice is nearly impossible. You are left with almost no time to intercept the input before it produces a bad outcome. This is why you have tried and failed so many times in the past when trying to fix this on your own.

God is going to have to do a work of grace inside your flesh to slow those responses down before you even have the option of making a good choice. Recognizing the problem and then acknowledging it as sin are going to begin the process God uses to slow down those signals. Eventually, as the work of sanctification happens inside, you will reach a point where you can submit yourself to the Spirit's control by making some necessary choices. Until then you're going to need to move on to trusting God and come back to making good choices after He has begun His work of sanctification.

Trust

Fixing conditioned responses yourself is *nearly* impossible, but it is not *completely* impossible. Not for God, who created the whole system in the first place. Since these are not biologically hard-wired reflexes that get intercepted in your spinal cord, the neurological signal that produces the conditioned response does pass through the brain. This means you do have a chance.

Just recognizing the problem will start the process of slowing down the sequence. Though the time your brain spends analyzing this input is extremely brief, it does pass through—sort of like a traveling businessman calling in to the office just to check messages. The next time the signal flies through your brain, it will find some new information waiting there: "This response is wrong."

With this your brain will have to pause, if even for a fraction of a second, to at least consider this new bit of information. The more often your brain makes that pause, the more it will slow down, making the change more likely. Plasticity will allow it to adapt and reconfigure the pathway.

This is what God is doing to intervene in your times of struggling. He is at work sanctifying these sin-sick nerve pathways to slow them down as you pray and ask Him for help. He may correct them supernaturally all at once as you open yourself completely to His healing work. In other areas, you may find you like your conditioned responses and choose to hold on to them. In those places God will bring times of struggling to help you let go. The pain you experience will help to break the power of these conditioned responses.

It won't work to try to just clamp down on your external behaviors. So long as the fleshly conditioned responses are still in control under the surface, clamping down won't fix anything. As God intervenes beneath the surface to change the automated responses, your resultant behaviors will change naturally.

Eventually the input signal will be slowed down to the point where you can consciously think about your options. Now it is time to go back to the submitting step and make a choice. This is where we ask questions like, "What would Jesus do?" Listen to God's still, small voice, and alter your behaviors appropriately.

Stand firm

It may take some time for God to slow down the signal long enough to allow you to deal with it on the conscious level. The frustrating thing is that after that difficult process, you are really just at the beginning, because now you have to start making good choices and changing your problem responses. But at least now you can begin the work—and allow Jesus Christ to begin it in you. Before, you were going straight to sin without even thinking about it.

The great thing about this process is that you can begin to make reflex-like responses for good decisions. Make the right choice enough times, and you won't even have to think about it the next time. It becomes automatic. It may take a while for this to happen. Don't get discouraged if this struggle drags on. Keep praying and trusting in God to change you from the inside out. Then go back to admitting and submitting what He shows you needs to change.

CHAPTER 7

SENSES—LIVING JUST TO STIMULATE YOUR RECEPTORS

Let's check in with Becky and Todd.

Becky

Becky's not doing too well these days. First, she broke off her engagement. Then her mom wasn't there for her when she needed her—she was off with Rick, Becky's evil brother. Now Rick is getting preferential treatment one more time by getting to stay at their parents' house at Thanksgiving.

Sure, why not? Give him everything. I'll just sit here in my tiny apartment and eat turkey from a frozen TV dinner. You won't even miss me. "Didn't there use to be somebody else at these gatherings?" "No, I don't think so." "Oh, OK. Never mind."

Speaking of dinner...

Becky's been hitting the fridge a lot lately. It's Wal-Mart's fault for putting ice cream on sale: buy two, get one free. After one of her binges, she always feels terrible. She punishes herself ruthlessly with all kinds of negative self-talk. But nothing seems to curb the behavior. She's already breaking out the larger-sized clothes she keeps in the closet for such times. Rick calls them her "whale clothes."

With that thought ringing in her brain, she makes a date with her two favorite men—Ben & Jerry—and sidles up to the table with a spoon. There's no explaining it, but when she's about a third of the way through a pint of Chunky Monkey, her troubles are replaced by sweet sensations. For the space of the remainder of the carton she is in bliss, enjoying a satisfied fullness. Her pulse is no longer racing. Her mind has left the speedway, and she is transported to a happy world of contentment and forgetfulness.

Reality is waiting for her at the bottom of the carton, along with hateful self-recriminations and a fear of the bathroom mirror. But the moment of sweet release makes it almost worth the price.

Todd

Todd works at a computer all day. He has his own office—with a door and everything. Sometimes he takes a break from his work to check the news online. His favorite source is Foxnews.com. You know, all the news, fair and balanced.

Today when he checks the news, an advertisement in the margin catches his eye. The new *Sports Illustrated* Swimsuit Edition is out. There's one of the oh-my-goodness models in a revealing bikini right there on the ad. He came to read about the Middle East, and now he's confronted with an image of an almost nude, beautiful woman. He feels his heart begin to beat faster. A pleasurable warmth starts at the back of his neck and rises up to his head. Everything in him is screaming for more images like that. Almost before he knows what he's doing, he's clicked on the ad.

But what's this? Instead of more soft porn, he's given a sign-up window to subscribe to *Sports Illustrated*. That was a mean trick. The heat coursing through his body starts to falter. No! Must maintain that feeling! So he does a quick search for "sports illustrated swimsuit edition" and finds a site showing last year's models. Who cares that they're not this year's—just look at them! His mouth drops open. *Wow.* Even as he gazes at their bodies, he feels a deep sense of guilt. What's more, he knows he's cheating his employer out of work time. But he doesn't care right now. It's been days since he's looked at any pornography, and this feels so, so good.

Used to be, even something this "soft-core" would give him a pretty good rush. Now it does very little for him. The

Senses—Living Just to Stimulate Your Receptors

women have some scraps of clothes on, after all. Even now the impact of these photos is beginning to lessen. If only the company didn't have those porn filters on the network, then he could really rock and roll.

Tonight, after everyone's asleep, I know what I'll be doing.

Good Vibes, Baby

If it feels good, do it. That seems to be the motto of our society. Everywhere you go, something appeals to your senses: beautiful models sporting expensive clothes (scant though they may be), amazing music from high-end stereos, exotic aromas wafting from nearby restaurants, and more. Marketers have figured out that the way to your heart (and checkbook) is through your senses. Remember our theory that God actually created the physical world to appeal to us through our senses. Senses are perhaps the most powerful forces impacting our flesh. And why not? Without them we really would have no life at all.

Can you imagine what it would be like to have no senses? It's tough enough to be blind or deaf, but I want you to imagine what it would be like to have none of your five major senses. What would it be like? Could you even live? How would you find food if you couldn't see or smell it? I guess you could grope around on the ground until you felt it—but wait, no sense of touch, either! You couldn't talk with people because you couldn't hear what they were saying. You really couldn't interact with anyone or anything at all.

See what I mean? Your senses define your every experience and therefore define your life. The majority of your life is spent gathering sensations and responding. Remember the neurologic pathways? Every single one in your body begins with some type of sensory input.

Could your life really be so base and meaningless? Perhaps you thought that human life was about grand themes like love defeating hate, faithfulness overcoming disloyalty, or kindness rising over brutality. And it certainly is, but without your senses you could not define any of these majestic concepts.

How could you? Without the ability to interact with other humans, these concepts would be meaningless. You could never understand the depths of committed love without watching a husband gently stroking the hand of his wife of sixty years as she lies dying, for example. You could never understand human brutality without having once felt the stinging pain of a violent blow or hearing someone's anguished cry.

Senses are not just the spice of life, as some have said. They *are* your life in the flesh.

Red Alert

Let's go back for just a minute to our old friends, the neurologic pathways. Stimuli enter our awareness through the senses. That's the receiving step in the process. The technical term for the entry point of these stimuli is *sensory receptor*. Every signal that travels to the brain to be analyzed and responded to begins at some type of sensory receptor.

Sensory receptors can be thought of like a smoke alarm in a building. They are positioned in spots where they are likely to detect smoke if there should be a fire. When smoke triggers a "receptor" in the smoke detector, a signal travels through a wire to the central security office where a security guard (the "brain" of the neurologic pathway) decides what to do. He *analyzes* the type of alarm that has activated, and, upon identifying it as a smoke detector, he *responds* by calling the fire department. Pretty simple, really. But your body has millions of these input fibers coming from dozens of different types of receptors, all converging on the brain.

Many of these input signals will come from the major senses: taste, touch, sight, smell, and hearing. These stimuli are detected by the appropriate types of receptors in the tongue, skin, eyes, nose, or ears, which send signals describing your surroundings back to the brain. Your body keeps track of what's going on around you using these senses.

But your body receives and analyzes many more sensations all day long. The diluteness of your blood, your blood pressure, temperature, and concentrations of numerous chemicals (just to name a few) all have specific sensory receptors that send signals to your brain when they are triggered by some stimulation.

But just having a signal enter the brain doesn't produce the "sensation" you ultimately feel. Your brain still has to analyze the input signal, and this analysis has a great deal to do with what sensation you eventually experience.

When someone rubs your back, for instance, many receptors in your skin and muscles send signals to the brain. Your touch, pressure, temperature, and even pain receptors are being stimulated, but the end result is not simply an acknowledgment of someone touching your back—it is a feeling of pleasure and relaxation. Even the mild pain signals sent to your brain during a vigorous massage don't cause alarm, but instead they can be enjoyable.

How do responses of enjoyment or relaxation come from simply being touched? The key is what happens in the analysis phase of the process. Past experiences and learned responses are combined during the analysis step of the pathway to create an emotionally charged response (pleasure) to the stimuli received by the skin. In this way your senses have a very powerful impact on your life.

Can't Get Enough

The problem comes when we go from *enjoying* the pleasurable responses to sensory input to *living for* those pleasurable responses.

Eating tasty foods, smelling nice perfume, and enjoying sexual touch are all popular ways to stimulate the senses for the purpose of pleasure. People go after cigarettes, drugs, and alcohol to get the pleasurable responses they produce. You can even get to the point that the desire for pleasurable sensations dominates your life. For some people, riding the sensory high is what life is all about.

When you do something that results in a strongly positive sensation, your flesh is prone to want to do that thing again. And again. It makes sense that pleasurable sensations, like the heart-pounding excitement of romance, would get the flesh begging for more. But even not-so-pleasurable stimuli, like horror movies or jumping out of airplanes, are craved by the flesh.

Why? Because all of these stimuli trigger the body's stress response, which in the absence of a real crisis can be quite enjoyable.

Recall how the stress hormone epinephrine, also known as adrenaline, raises heart rate and blood pressure, reduces pain sensations, and heightens other sensations by increasing blood flow to the brain. This gives us the "rush" we enjoy during these exciting activities.

There is a problem, however. While you are enjoying this rush of sensation, your body is still trying to maintain that constant state of normalcy called homeostasis. When you are plummeting down the side of a mountain while snowboarding, your body will turn down, or "down-regulate," the thrill sensations so it won't be so overwhelmed if the situation happens again. In fact, any stimuli that are extreme or overused will be down-regulated by your body in time.

This includes the five major senses. During my medical training I was taught how to perform autopsies. As you can imagine, the first day in the morgue the smell was overpowering. The instructor chuckled and said, "You'll get used to it." I didn't believe him. But sure enough, in a day or so I hardly noticed the smell. Why? The odors were so strong that my sense of smell was getting overloaded, so the olfactory (sense of smell) centers in my brain were turned down to avoid overstimulation.

What your body is doing when it down-regulates a neurologic pathway is actually adjusting the strength of the sensation that is produced after a receptor is triggered. In other words, it's turning down the volume. The stereo is still playing—it's just not as loud. The result is that you don't have the same level of reaction to something that had once overwhelmed your senses. This is a good thing if it allows you to perform an autopsy without being blown away by the smell. But if you're trying to repeat the buzz from your first glass of wine, you may not think that this down-regulation is such a good thing. Your brain has reset the scales a bit, so it will be that much harder—and take that much more alcohol—to achieve the same buzz next time.

And that is how addictions are born.

As a person discovers that he enjoys a certain stimulus, he pursues it more and more. The more he indulges in it, however, the more his body down-regulates the response to try and maintain normalcy, which means he will have to get more and more stimuli to feel the same effect.

Let's look at alcohol's effects a little closer. While it's producing the pleasurable "buzz" or "high" feelings, alcohol is also causing a decrease in heart rate, muscular activity, and mental activity. So as alcohol enters, suppressing these systems, the body responds by increasing heart rate, muscular activity, and mental activity. It's fighting to not get drunk, in other words. It's working to maintain homeostasis. What this means to the drinker is that more alcohol will be needed to produce the same response next time. Give the body more alcohol, and it will produce more suppression, resulting in a need for even more alcohol. So goes the cycle of addiction.

If someone drinks daily, the constant supply of alcohol requires a constant countering force by the body to allow him to feel normal. There is a new "normal," one that can only be maintained by more alcohol.

You can see the body's countering force in action by suddenly removing the suppressive effects of the alcohol. This leaves the underlying increase in bodily functions unmasked. The heightened heart rate, muscular activity, and mental activity would be unopposed, resulting in rapid heart rate, convulsions, and hallucinations—common symptoms of delirium tremens, or "DTs," as the person withdraws from the effects of the alcohol. The body's countering effects to strong stimuli are so strong that, as in this case, they can be life threatening.

Over a period of time without alcohol, the body's regulatory systems will eventually readjust their levels of function back to normal. Even with the worst kind of addictions, it is possible to return the body to balance.

"But I'm Not an Addict"

When it comes to drugs and alcohol, addiction is well understood. But we can also become controlled by other things we indulge in. Indeed, any sensory stimulation we experience excessively can become an addiction in a sense when the flesh is regulating it.

Todd likes to indulge his visual senses by looking at pornography. Well, what he really likes are the internal sensations of pleasure that shoot through his body when he's doing so. Sexual activity and viewing pornographic material cause the body to release sexual hormones and adrenaline. The physical responses from these chemicals are extremely pleasurable, so we seek repeated stimulation. But the body counters the overstimulation by down-regulating the pathways controlling the sensations. That means that more and more stimulation is required to produce the desired response—and the person is hooked.

People who indulge in activities like pornography and illicit sexual activity are doing so to get a "high" from the sensations. They're actually using the chemicals produced by their body to produce a pleasurable feeling, much in the same way that a heroine addict abuses a chemical by injection.

What's the difference between picking up a magazine to cause the release of a chemical from inside the body (like testosterone or adrenaline) and picking up a syringe to inject a chemical from outside the body (like heroin)? Both are addictions to a chemical, and both result from the flesh's lust for stimulation.

And it's not just the feelings released by sex and pornography that we can get hooked on. You'd be surprised what our fleshly desire for sensory stimulation can make us addicted to. Joggers and weightlifters, for instance, have been shown to become addicted to endorphins, chemicals that are internally released during exercise. Some eating disorders act very much like an addiction.

Look at Becky's plunge into the Ben & Jerry's ice cream. She turns to the sensation of taste when she needs pleasurable sensations to counter the bad feelings produced by her family. It is not just the taste sensations that she's yearning for. She wants help in dealing with her anxiety. When we're stressing out, eating is one way to stimulate a whole system of nerves and hormones in the parasympathetic nervous system that work in an opposite way from the fight-or-flight response. These produce what we call the "rest-and-regurgitation" response.

The parasympathetic neurologic pathways are stimulated after *eating* because they direct energy toward digestion and away from other bodily functions—like thought and muscular activity. In other words, eating sets off a whole neurologic process designed to relax us. We've all experienced this. How many people push away from the table and end up snoozing on the couch in front of the TV? After you eat, your pulse slows, your intestines give you a quiet rumble of contentment, and your mind drifts away from the stresses of life and into a state of calm.

You can see how people can become addicted to that kind of peacefulness, especially if their lives are full of the opposite. But it's still an addiction, which means the flesh is ruling them at that point.

Researchers believe that addictions to drugs like tobacco, cocaine, and heroin may all happen because they eventually stimulate the release of *dopamine*. Dopamine and other neurotransmitters like it that have powerful effects on the brain are not released only by addictive drugs. Many other kinds of stimuli cause them to be released. It is conceivable that the stimulation from other things that can control us—like pride, greed, resentment, or materialism—may also cause dopamine to be released, with similar results. With repeated stimulation and the body's resulting down-regulation, we can become dependent on these internal chemicals, leading us to be addicted to these behaviors.

So you might be more of an addict than you think. It's no wonder that kicking the habit of pride or bitterness can sometimes be just as difficult as getting free from drugs.

Help for All Us Addicts

Have you ever seen a daytime television show where husbands were using so-called "sexual addictions" as an excuse for their multiple extramarital affairs? If so, you probably said what I said: "What a cop-out!" Well, now you know there might just be some truth in their argument. As we realize how powerful our fleshly senses are, we begin to see that *all of us* are addicted to sensory input in our flesh.

Don't get me wrong: this doesn't excuse bad behavior. I think there is a real danger in labeling these behaviors as *addictions* if doing so somehow makes them excusable. And we should not use such a statement to suggest that there is no solution for the problem simply because we have an "addictive personality." Sin is still sin, even if there's a fleshly impulse behind it.

The important thing to grasp in all of this is that *the flesh craves sensory stimulation*. That's what it lives for. If it could have its way, we would bounce from stimulation to stimulation, never coming down from the pleasurable plateau of constant sensory input. When the flesh is in control, life is spent searching for the next fix of sensory stimulation.

In fact, that's how many of us actually live. We go through each day with one purpose: to look for new ways to stimulate our receptors. It could be with drugs, sex, and alcohol, or just as easily with pride, power, and influence. Or it might be with fine music, expensive jewelry, or extreme sports. Maybe we're hooked on the rush we get when we receive positive strokes from people we admire. Whatever makes us feel good and gives us that rush of sensation, this is what our flesh loves.

Is it evil to seek enjoyment? Is it wrong to have influence or own things? No, but it is *fleshly*. And if you give yourself over to the flesh's control, you will quickly find yourself in bondage, with sin and damage pouring out in your life.

With chemical addictions it is easy to see the bondage at work. People continue to pursue the chemical they are addicted to despite its damage to their health. Remember those smokers I told you about who quit after having a major illness? The amazing thing is that they are only the smart ones. As many as 50 percent of smokers will continue smoking after a heart attack, even though they know it will worsen their heart condition. Addictions are powerful and destructive.

The bondage that comes from addiction to non-chemical sensory pleasures isn't as easy to spot, but you will end up in bondage and struggling just the same. Why? Because you will always need more. You will never get enough stimulation to make your flesh happy once and for all. Just when you think you are almost getting there, your sensations will be down-regulated, and you will be left searching for your next fix of sensation.

Sensory Addicts Anonymous

Since all of us have a flesh that craves sensory stimulation, I'm willing to assume that you've been reading this chapter very carefully, that perhaps you've even seen yourself in these pages. In fact, it is quite likely that the recurring sin in your life that made you pick

SENSES—LIVING JUST TO STIMULATE YOUR RECEPTORS

up this book in the first place is in some measure related to the pleasurable sensations it gives you. The reason you can't ever beat this thing is that, on some level, *it feels really good.*

So it's time to admit it—you're an addict. A rush junkie. In your flesh you crave and can't live without some good feeling you're getting from your sin. Even though somewhere deep inside it feels good, your addiction is screwing up your life. It is causing you to struggle. You need treatment.

TREATMENT PLAN

Listen

If you want to identify where fleshly sensory addiction may be controlling your life, start by examining the situation you are struggling with. What kind of rush do you find yourself trying to get? Where are you driven to stimulate a sensory response to feel good? Can you spot it happening in you? Where are your decisions being made and actions being carried out just to get that next taste, touch, smell, sight, or sound? What do you do to get that next pleasurable shot of adrenaline, sexual buzz, or feeling of respect—or any other sensory response?

When you learn to see *where* you're trying to get those rushes, you're ahead of the game. But you can also try to see *when* you're trying to get those rushes. When you feel that fever begin to come over you, that pressure to do the thing that will trigger the buzz, try to just stop and take a snapshot of what's going on.

Can you hardly wait until the weekend to get out on your mountain bike and go flying down the side of a hill? Has it become every weekend now, even though you told your wife it would be only once a month? Do you get a thrill catching men's eyes? When you walk past a certain young man's cubicle, can you almost not resist stopping by or "accidentally" drawing his attention somehow? If you can spot the when of it, you can figure out the why of it, and you'll be close to your goal.

When the flesh is addicted to a sensation, you will feel a sense of pressure deep inside. It is that thing that seems to take over your hand, and all of a sudden you have your wallet out and are handing over your credit card because your eyes saw something nice in a store. Your flesh says, "Just buy it. You've had a tough week, and this will make you feel good."

This pressure comes because your body's regulatory systems have gotten used to having a constant supply of the stimulation you are addicted to. When the level of this stimulation drops off, your body's altered state becomes apparent—you feel like you desperately need a fix—and you are driven to do the thing that will generate the stimulation again. Only this time you'll have to get more stimulation to achieve the same high, because your body has down-regulated.

What about this: Are you drawn to sit in front of the TV for hours at a time watching all the pretty people and experiencing all the drama, while meanwhile your family goes about their lives without you? Have you let the bills pile up because you'd rather go golfing? Another tip-off that you may have a sensory addiction is when you find yourself neglecting other important things in order to get your fix and restore the feeling of balance in your body, just as an alcoholic does.

But you say you need to zone out a little by watching TV at night to relax? Or the golf you play is good for your health and business connections? Sounds surprisingly like the alcoholic who told me he needed alcohol to help him relax, or the drug addict who said coke helped him tune out the world for a while.

None of these activities are wrong by themselves. But if they captivate your thinking, monopolize your time, and drag you away from other priorities, they are in control. If you find you have an area like this in your life, this is the place that needs sanctification.

The God issue with sensory addictions may be the most important of them all. Remember why we said God put us in this physical world with all of its fleshly pleasures? To choose Him instead. We need to realize that our flesh just loves sensory stimulation. The God issue here is whether or not we love this world more than we love God. What pleasures would you give up to follow Him? Thankfully He doesn't require sacrifice (Psalm 51:16) to prove our love, but He does yearn for hearts that desire Him. Consider your love for the sensations of this world as you probe the depths of your flesh in this area.

Admit

Treatment for addiction to fleshly sensations starts much in the same way you treat addictions to external chemicals. The very first step is that you have to admit you're an addict. You have to stand up and say, "Hi, my name is Bob, and I'm a sensoryholic." (Hello, Bob.) You have to admit that in your flesh you are addicted to the good sensation you get from your particular sin and that it's messing up your life, and you have to admit that this is wrong and needs to change.

I can imagine someone asking me: "What's so bad about being addicted to a pleasurable sensation, so long as I keep it under control?" Hello! You're being lied to. You've bought into the flesh's line, the one it uses to retain its control in your life. Thinking you can control your fleshly addictions is as dangerous as it is impossible.

Let's talk about gambling, for example. The thrill of gambling is attractive to some who say they're playing it "just as a game" and claim it can be kept under control. But many of these same people have lost their homes and families to a gambling addiction. Drugs and alcohol are the same way. So many drug and alcohol fatalities involve people who would have said their use of it was under control: "I can stop whenever I want to."

Your flesh likes the rush you get from the addiction. By shifting what it considers "normal," it has come to need it. So it is certainly going to feed you all kinds of lines to keep you giving it what it craves. It will also work very hard to protect its flow of the good stuff if you begin threatening to cut it off.

Any addiction, whether it be to the drug called Ecstasy or the drug called hatred, or even the drug called admiration, is bondage and should not be toyed with. It is dangerous to think you can control the flesh's addictions. Just when you think you have it under control, you find that the flesh is actually controlling you!

A worse problem than gambling is simple materialism. Throwing money away on the thrill of buying things has probably destroyed more people financially than gambling. Materialism is far more common—just as gluttony and the obesity it produces are a far greater health problem in our country than illicit drug use because of the number of the people they affect. Millions of us are trying to feed the flesh's craving for stimulation and ending up being trapped by it. And once you are trapped by the flesh, it will set out to destroy you.

Admitting that you like your particular fleshly addiction even though you know it is hurting you is the beginning of freedom. Many times we continue to struggle because even though we know a particular thing might be wrong, we secretly love the feelings it gives us and don't want them to end. The result is that on the outside you yell, "I hate this sin! God, free me from it," while on the inside you scream, "I love this sin! God, I want to keep it." This is the conflict Paul spoke of in Romans 6–7.

Of course, God hears both of these messages. He hears the prayer, but He also sees you holding on to the sin with both hands. He won't tear out of your grasp something you want to hang on to. What He will do, though, is send a little struggling to loosen your grip.

You may be uncomfortable with the idea of God sending struggling into your life. But remember, He is a loving Father who will use chastisement if necessary to get you to turn from the flesh and back to Him.

If you would like, you can view it simply as your sin leading to consequences. But the struggling doesn't always clearly match the sin, which can lead to some of the most confusing and difficult times of struggling. A spouse may leave—due in no part to relational problems in your life—when God is getting you to make Him your first love. You may be a great employee, but lose your job unfairly as God dries up the finances to deal with a hidden materialism. And sometimes, it's actually someone else's flesh hurting your life. You're not the only one who could be ruled by the flesh, after all.

The bottom line is that God is sovereign. Whether the hardship comes as a consequence of your sin, someone else's sin, or even God's direct action, it doesn't truly matter. His primary goal is to subdue your flesh, and He'll sacrifice your fleshly comforts if that's what it takes to accomplish that goal.

When you are dealing with addiction to sensory stimulation, the struggle God sends will usually result in your sin not being so pleasurable anymore. What once gave you enjoyable sensations will now give you painful feelings, until finally it will be a relief to let go.

Admitting you are wrong in this case requires rejecting the pleasure of the sin to the point where you no longer see the stimulation as a good thing. This is what God is trying to accomplish through your struggling. Once you have attained this, the power of your addiction will be broken.

Submit

The next step in dealing with an addiction is to stop indulging in it. In that brief moment of choice, you exercise a minute amount of power to choose to take the narrow road. As you make these tiny turns away from the sensations your flesh is addicted to, the Spirit regains control, and your body's regulatory functions begin to return to normal. This takes time and much support, and—don't miss this—it will result in a period of significant struggling as you withdraw from this difficult problem in your life. You'll find yourself going through DTs just like the alcoholic—not delirium tremens, just very difficult times.

Making the choice to turn down the opportunity to enjoy your vice is best done by turning down the opportunity to even get into the situation where your vice is offered. This means if alcohol is a problem, you start by choosing not to go into places where they serve alcohol so you are never presented with the choice of whether to drink or not. Don't drive past the strip joints. Don't "drop by" the ice cream shop. Don't go into the convenience store where those magazines are available for flipping through.

In the past I used to "shoot up" with the thrill I felt in the praise of men. I could get a pretty good hit from teaching a class or leading some group at church. Eventually I felt it was interfering with my motives for ministry, so I decided to go cold turkey and stay out of the limelight for a while. My pastor thought it was a little odd that I turned down his request to give the Sunday morning offertory prayer, but I wanted to avoid going to a place where my vice was offered—which in this case was up in front of church people. So I chose to spend some time in kitchen ministry and stay away from "up front" ministries until God had brought this craving under control.

Trust

As I said, the first step to beating your addiction to sensory input is choosing to remove the stimulation. But that is not enough to conquer the flesh in this area. Selling your computer to get rid of Internet porn is not going to fix your problem completely. You can go "cold turkey" and remove your favorite stimulation, but it will not remove the flesh's desire buried deep inside.

The ultimate solution is to change what the flesh in you desires. But guess what: this is something you can't do on your own; it takes the power of the Holy Spirit. Once again we see that sanctification does not occur by just trying harder. The flesh itself must be changed. This requires God's sovereign work in you as you commit yourself to His process of sanctification.

Pray that He does a work inside of you to bring your craving for sensory stimulation under control, and trust that He will do it.

Stand firm

Like any junkie coming out of a habit, you are going to need to spend some time in rehab. In this case that means an admission to God's spiritual detox center, where you will be treated with prayer, worship, the study of His Word, and fellowship until your flesh "dries out." Be diligent with the disciplines of Christianity to strengthen your spirit as you fight against your flesh.

Once you have recognized the sensory stimulation you crave, you have identified the enemy; now it is time for a war of attrition. You starve him out. This may mean cutting off your flesh's access to the sensory stimulation it loves. If you are dealing with the thrill that materialism provides, you need to not only stay out of the stores, you also need to throw away the catalogues and maybe even turn off the TV to avoid the enticing advertisements.

If pornography is an issue for you, it is time to also stay away from R-rated movies and even television shows, which these days are sexually explicit enough to provide sensual stimulation. And don't get me started on beer commercials.

Are you toying with the excitement of considering an extramarital affair? It is time to stop hanging out with the non-Christian friends after work. You might even want to avoid a few of the folks at church. And don't invite that "friend" from the opposite sex out for lunch to help "support" you during your marital problems. You're playing with fire and setting yourself up for failure. You're going to have to have to limit the amount of input you get from members of the opposite sex if that is stimulating you toward sin. And, oh yeah, I almost forgot, turn off the TV, which is constantly depicting the excitement and the lack of negative consequences from extramarital sexual activity.

Is it just me, or are we beginning to detect a trend here? There's a connection between television and fleshly sensory addiction. The tube is probably the single biggest source of sensory input for your flesh. Watching it is like hooking your flesh up to an I.V. and pumping it full of nutrition. If you are fighting a war of attrition with your flesh, you are going to have to turn off the TV.

Change does not come overnight, and in some cases it never comes completely. Just as most alcoholics need to keep a lifelong goal of abstinence, your area of addiction may require a lifetime of standing firm. But as you do, the Lord will defeat the power of your flesh. And that means you'll be walking more and more in the Spirit.

CHAPTER 8

SUBCONSCIOUS BRAIN FUNCTIONS—PROGRAMMED TO BE ME

CAMILLE

Family night. Ugh. The night Bob makes the whole family get into the van and go out to eat. And every time they have the same problem in the car—where would they go to eat?

"I want a happy meal at McDonald's!" shouts Josh, the youngest.

"No way," Camille says. "I'm not in the mood for grease tonight."

"How about pizza?" Ashley suggests. "That's quick. And then you could drop me off at the mall!"

"Nope," Camille says, changing lanes suddenly. "We did pizza for lunch at work this week, and I just couldn't do it again. And forget going to the mall." *If I have to suffer, then everyone else will suffer with me.*

"Oh, Mom!"

Bob, the peacemaker, looks over from the passenger seat and tries to spot the common ground among the variety of opinions. "We haven't done Chinese for a long time. What do you say?"

"Why do you do that?" Camille asks. "You know I don't like Chinese. You're always suggesting things I don't like."

And so it goes for a few more rounds. Camille vetoes everyone's suggestions until they finally ask her where she wants to go. Dino's, a nice place near her office. They have good mahi there, and she was having a craving.

"Well, OK," Bob says doubtfully. "But I heard they've upped their prices again. Why don't we look for someplace less—"

"So what if they've raised their prices a couple of bucks?" Camille says. "You're such a penny-pincher, Bob. Live a little, why don't you? Look, you and I both work so that we can have a few extras now and then, right? And you know what a week I had at work this time. I deserve grilled mahi, and that's what I'm going to have."

She parks the car—across two spaces—and all but jogs toward the door to get their names on the list ahead of anyone else. She spots a woman headed for the door. How can she beat her without breaking into a run? She walks as fast as her legs can carry her, but it's not going to be fast enough.

Just before the other woman reaches the door, she twists her ankle on the step and falls with a yelp. She sprawls on the red carpet, her shoulder scraping against a stone trash can and the sleeve of her dress ripping.

Out loud, Camille says, "Oh! Are you all right?" But inside she's thinking, *Too bad for you, honey.* As she steps in to get her name on the list, she says, "I'll get someone to help you."

ALEX

Alex delivers parts to auto repair shops. If a mechanic needs a new carburetor or CV joint, he calls the parts store and the parts store sends Alex to deliver. Alex buzzes all over town, up one road down the next. Past billboard after billboard strategically placed to fill in the gaps between concrete walls in case any open airspace might show through. On the radio one DJ after another drones along, fighting back any silence that attempts to sneak into his truck.

All day long ads are pulling at his eyes and ears trying to draw his attention to an endless display of things to improve his life. Adding to the background clutter, in shop after shop there are nudie calendars splashed around the walls, and the chainsaw melodies of Metallica are filling his ears as he fills the shelves.

After winding his way through this maze, Alex will often arrive home stressed and anxious. Maybe tonight will

Subconscious Brain Functions—Programmed to Be Me

be like the others. Nothing particular will be wrong; there will just be that dull ache behind his right eye that seems to make everything at home tough to deal with at night. Finally his wife's voice droning in the background will be the last straw. He'll snap and head out to someplace quiet to get a drink.

On this particular day Alex does his usual route, but this time with the additional stop at the garage down by the Pleasure Palace strip club. He's a little extra tense and comes home from work almost desperate for sex with his wife. He has no idea why—and she's not willing to comply.

What is wrong with that woman? He thinks as he slips out for another nightcap to help him calm the tumult of the day.

You've Got Issues

These two stories don't appear to have much in common with one another, except perhaps that if you knew either Alex or Camille you would probably say, "Man, do they have issues!"

And it's true; they have some deep-seated issues that make up who they are as people. Camille is a bit selfish, a little controlling, and, well, downright nasty. Alex is a little tense, maybe a little introverted, and not a great communicator. They both probably have some underlying depression. Alex, as we will see, is affected by things his subconscious mind has detected but that haven't registered with him consciously. Camille is only acting the way her subconscious has predisposed her to act. The common denominator is that both are struggling because of something going on in their subconscious brain centers.

We all have some powerful influences from our subconscious brain centers, which means very likely you and I have some issues, too.

Subconscious Brain Centers

There are many neurologic functions that happen without us thinking consciously about them. Did you know that roughly 80 percent of your brain is permanently committed to the tons of processing that goes on somewhere below the level of conscious thought? So even though it seems like your whole life is lived in a world where you can think about and respond to every issue that affects you, this is only a small part of reality. The vast majority of your brainpower—all the sensing, analyzing, and responding—is being used to deal with things subconsciously.

The most basic of these subconscious centers deal with the most basic functions. Things you probably associate with the subconscious, like breathing and heart rate and other organ function. But there are many other subconscious brain functions that have a direct affect on the way you live and may contribute to the things that make you struggle.

We are going to look at just a few interesting aspects of the subconscious areas of your brain to demonstrate how they work together to produce the style and personality that makes you, you. The neurologic processes of the brain are incredibly complex, however, and I can definitely be accused of oversimplifying them here. If you want to learn more, you will have to do additional reading.

Deep in the brain the *basal ganglia* are primarily responsible for coordinating your movements. It is here that it is decided whether you are smooth and svelte, or a klutz. The basal ganglia also control the timed events in life. You did not decide you were emotionally ready for puberty when it happened; your basal ganglia decided for you that it was time and that you would have dramatic changes in the way you act and think—ready or not.

The built-in timer in the basal ganglia can also signal you when it's time to remember things like your anniversary. Let that one slip, and you may find out how severely these subconscious brain functions can impact your life!

Information storage is handled subconsciously in the *hippocampus*, the section of the brain that works along with other areas of the brain to produce memories. Little is known about how this works, but this important brain center is determining which events you will learn from and which will pass, forgotten, into oblivion. Are you the type to hold on to past hurts and resentments? It is probably decided more by your hippocampus than by you.

One of the more powerful subconscious areas is the *limbic system*, which attaches an emotion to the responses generated in other parts of the brain. As you are watching a movie, the death of a character may generate anger if he was the hero, or joy if the deceased was the villain. The emotional response that is appropriate will be determined in the limbic system.

We'll talk in more detail about the complexities of this system in the next chapter, but an important point is that this subconscious brain center is interconnected with nearly every other response pathway. This means that there is an emotional impact from almost every stimulus received and every response you give. You may not feel them all consciously, but all of these tiny subconscious emotional stimuli are adding pressure and intensity to the way you respond throughout the day.

It's All About You

So now that you know all of this subconscious stuff is going on, you may be asking how any of it affects you. The answer is that it doesn't just affect you—it is you. All of this subconscious processing and responding makes you uniquely you.

Is your cup half full or half empty? If it's half full, you're probably irritated by people like me who are usually half empty. I have to tell you honestly that you perky people irritate the rest of us. But we can't really be upset with each other. Your general mood is less about your outlook on life and more about your levels of dopamine and serotonin in your brain, which is demonstrated by the fact that most antidepressants and many other psychiatric medications are designed to alter these neurotransmitters.

In fact, your whole personality really is the sum total of all of these processes churning away below the surface. And this is a good thing. It is the way God has designed us all to be different people instead of stamped-out carbon copies.

As you are examining your life for problems with the flesh, you cannot forget all these important physical processes that shape the way you respond to situations in life based on your personality. In fact, if you would like to do a little self-analysis in this area, there are a number of interesting descriptions of our personalities that have been done that can help you understand how your fleshly tendencies will make you respond.

My favorite is a personality profile used by Marita Littauer and Florence Littauer; it is an expansion of work done by Tim LaHaye.

They describe four personalities, and you will find that even though you may be a mix, one or two will dominate your character.

Popular Sanguine is the creative, outspoken, encouraging type who likes to keep things humorous and playful, and gravitates toward the limelight. Their light-hearted nature makes them a little flighty, and they tend to be distracted and forgetful. These are the people who are great at a party—but don't let them balance your checkbook.

The Powerful Choleric personality is the born leader. They are decisive visionaries. They motivate others and are task-oriented. If you have a job to get done, you want to find a choleric personality, but be careful, because they tend to be bossy, impulsive, and intimidating. This is Camille from the restaurant scene, pushing her way through life. And if you just need compassion—forget it. They're more likely to be in your face than in your corner.

For compassion try the Peaceful Phlegmatic, who is more caring. But they tend to be the push-me-and-I'll-go type. Don't ask them to decide on a restaurant. Like Bob above, by the time they decide, you won't be hungry anymore. As hard as they are to motivate, however, they are also hard to rile up. They will be the ones to reach a compromise, stay calm in chaos, and stay committed for the long haul.

The perfectionist is the Perfect Melancholy. They are sensitive to people's need and are detail people who are great with numbers and planning. They like lists and defined goals. This makes them great people to have on your organization's management board, but they can sometimes become a stumbling block due to discouragement and even depression when things don't add up and every detail isn't perfect. And the same goes for imperfect people (including themselves), who usually get criticism rather than support and understanding.

Hippocrates, the father of medicine, was the first to suggest a link between personality and the brain. We still haven't pinpointed that one group of neurons that has been shown to make you one type of personality or another. It is more complicated than that. But the fact that these personality types have been so clearly defined in us tells us that they are preprogrammed. They are one more good thing that God has designed into our flesh to allow us to function in this world together.

Another thing to keep in mind is that not only do your subconscious systems make you, you, but also they are *all about you!* Every system in your body is designed to provide for you, to keep you alive and in a happy state of homeostasis. The flesh is always looking out for #1. In short, you are programmed in your flesh to be selfish.

The benefit is that this is the way God made you to be able to acquire what you need to survive. The downside is that there is nothing in all of your fleshly processes that is designed to spontaneously provide for the concerns of anyone else. That makes you and me, in our flesh, inherently selfish. And *that* is not how God wants us to remain.

We can see this happening in our story about Camille. Her flesh is in control of her actions, so her actions are designed to meet her needs only, without regard to others. She wants what she wants, frankly, because she wants it. And she wants it first, faster, and for free.

Since selfishness is the result of things happening in your mind on a subconscious level, you can find yourself acting selfishly before your conscious mind is even called into action. Your conscious mind may have the chance to intervene later, tempering the selfishness so as to include other people's needs. But as far as your subconscious mind is concerned, it's all about you.

Something Has Gone Wrong

When everything is working well, your subconscious centers take pretty good care of you. Your subconscious brain is an incredibly complex machine that manages all of the data regarding your sensations, memories, and emotions pretty smoothly most of the time.

It is roughly like a sophisticated computer humming along, managing all of your body's functions. Just like a computer, your subconscious brain requires a significant number of parts, chemicals, and electrical signals working just right to make it work. In your brain, the parts are nerve cells, the chemicals are neurotransmitters, and the electrical signals travel along nerves not wires—but it is pretty similar to your PC.

And therein lies the problem. I'm sure your PC is just like mine, and that just like me, you have days when you absolutely hate it. It crashes. It freezes up. The printer stops working. The Internet bogs down. The modem doesn't connect. The fax won't transmit. And on and on. When computers work they are great, but when something goes wrong, it leaves you struggling.

Well, the same is true with your subconscious brain centers. Unfortunately, something has gone wrong with you. It is called the fall of man, when sin entered our world. Since then all types of problems have plagued mankind, not the least of which are the physical ailments that plague our bodies. When physical problems disrupt your subconscious brain centers, they can cause a whole list of problems that lead to struggling.

They could be as little as the nuances about your personality. This is why Bob from above is a little more passive and Camille a little more aggressive. Josh, the youngster, just wanted his happy meal. And Ashley, the teenager, wanted to get to the mall with her friends. Each of them was created differently in their flesh by God to be just who they were, and it is all good.

But problems can also be more severe. A malfunction in the hippocampus occurs, and you can't learn quite as well as the other kids. Mess with a few neurons, and schizophrenia can result. Change a few chemicals, and suddenly you're depressed. We live with a fallen, imperfect flesh, and when things inside our flesh don't work properly, it is going to affect our lives.

Subconscious Senses

I want to look now at one of the most important subconscious centers in your brain: the *thalamus*. The thalamus is where nearly all sensory input is brought first. The eyes see something, and the images are sent to the thalamus. The ears hear something, the tongue tastes something, etc.—all of that input is shuttled to the thalamus. The same goes for internal senses and anything else that may trigger a neurologic pathway. It all has to go to the thalamus first. It's the receiving area of the brain.

Subconscious Brain Functions—Programmed to Be Me

Again we are really simplifying here, but one of the jobs of the thalamus is to decide which signals can be handled at a subconscious, automated level, and what information needs to be sent "upstairs" for deliberation by the conscious mind.

It's something like my answering service. Calls come to the nice folks at my service, and they screen them before passing them on to me. If a patient needs an appointment, that gets handled automatically by a secretary without me ever knowing about it. If a patient has a question or needs a prescription, that will be forwarded to me at the next convenient time. If a patient is having an emergency, the call gets put through to me "stat."

Temperature regulation is a good example of how the thalamus works—and how it can send information to your conscious mind. All day long your body monitors temperature. When the temperature rises, sweat glands are activated and blood flow changes are made without your knowing it, in an attempt to cool your body. If the temperature falls, a shivering response is activated to help increase body temperature. Only if these mechanisms fail to solve the problem will your thalamus send the signal to the higher brain centers for additional responses to be generated.

Let's say you're asleep and it's starting to get cold. Your brain will signal your arms to pull the covers up. Your conscious mind will not even know of these external movements. If your body is still too cold, then and only then will your thalamus wake you up. It tells your conscious mind that it is time to get up and close the window.

Sensory Overload

It's not only about pulling up the covers while you sleep. Your subconscious, especially in how it handles sensory information, can have a profound effect on your everyday *waking* life by directing many of your actions.

Consider this example: have you ever tried to talk to a friend about an important issue in a noisy, crowded room? It's almost impossible, isn't it? Either you can't hear the important stuff because of all the noise in the room, or you're getting distracted by what else is going on. Either way, your conversation is failing. Perhaps you decide to step outside, away from the distraction.

Your subconscious centers were getting overloaded trying to sort through all of the background noise and still concentrate on the conversation, so your thalamus signaled you to move away from the distraction.

This kind of power surge of sensation happens to me when I'm at home trying to read while someone is listening to music in the background, the children are fighting in another room, the TV is on, and someone else is trying to talk to me. It finally gets to me, and I shout, "Sensory overload!" I have to turn off everything and everyone around me temporarily so that I can deal with them one at a time.

Well, your brain responds in the same way. It simply turns off some senses—it hits the mute button—so it can concentrate on other senses. Have you ever lost your glasses only to find that you had pushed them up and were wearing them atop your head? To help you concentrate on your search for the glasses, your body muted the sensory stimulation that was overwhelming you—including the sense of touch that was trying to tell you where they were.

Have you ever spoken to someone while he was doing something else, only to have him respond, "I'm sorry, did you say something?" His sense of hearing was temporarily turned off to help him concentrate on the task at hand. Even sight can be turned off. We have all observed people looking off in a blank stare and waved our hands in front of their eyes to get them to respond. The sense of sight was momentarily shut down to direct energy to their thoughts.

When your brain decides to "turn off" one of your senses, it's not really turning it off completely. It's simply leaving the sensory input down there in the subconscious part of the brain without bringing it up to the higher levels where it would be analyzed consciously. The information is still being sensed by the receptor, and it is still being received and analyzed by the brain; very often a response is being generated. It is just being done subconsciously and automatically. Your brain knows what's going on, but it's not telling you!

This explains why you can arouse someone out of a blank stare by waving your hand in front of his face. His eyes are still receiving information, even though he is not conscious of it. When a stimulus comes along that the brain feels the person should respond to (the hand waving), the thalamus diverts the information to the conscious levels of the brain where it is addressed. All the previous sights that the eyes viewed while the person was staring were also seen and evaluated, but they were determined to be not sufficiently important to pass on to higher levels. They were dealt with in the subconscious rather than being sent on to the conscious mind.

Well, here is the point of all of this: this is important because it means that there is a tremendous amount of information that is affecting you subconsciously without *you* knowing it. You may state adamantly that you are completely in control of all that you do, when really there is something below the surface affecting you in your flesh.

Have you ever gotten tense or agitated and have no idea why? It might be that you're being overstimulated by background noise. This happens to me in the operating room quite often when I am concentrating on a long operation and I begin to feel a growing sense of tension. I stop what I am doing and look around. Often someone has turned on the radio, and heavy metal music is playing in the background and affecting me subconsciously.

Receiving so much subconscious stimulation may result in subtle anxiety without an obvious source. This can make you react to people around you with frustrated or even angry responses, as Alex did earlier, without being aware of what is affecting you.

It is important to realize the profound effect that your subconscious brain centers, and also subconscious stimuli, have on your life. Your actions may be affected without you being aware of it.

Treatment Plan

Listen

Finding the effects of subconscious problems in your life is going to be tough. Why? Well, they're not called subconscious for nothing. They're below the level of conscious thought. However, there are a couple of things that can act like ripples on the surface of the water, tipping you off to the spot where a problem lies directly below the surface.

Let's start with the preprogrammed responses. This is the subconscious programming that makes you the person you are. Take a look at your life. What type of person are you? Consider taking a personality test.[1] This will help you understand how your flesh is predisposed to make you act. This isn't to identify a good or godly personality type or a sinful one. God made us all to be unique, and in His plan for creation, it is all good. There are positive and negative characteristics to each personality—unless, of course, the flesh is in full control.

Introverts may be more effective at intimate communication. If you want to share a personal problem, they're the ones to get with. They risk becoming isolated and ineffective, however, if their flesh is allowed to make them withdraw into themselves. If, on the other hand, you're planning an evangelistic crusade, you'll want to take advantage of an extrovert's gifts. Take that same personality in its unsanctified state to a party and give it a few drinks, and you'll find his friends cringing on the other side of the room hoping no one knows they're together.

The problems you are having with your wife may be due to the fact that you are just not a "touchy-feely person" by nature and her love language is physical closeness. When you find yourself saying, "Honey, I'm sorry I'm not meeting your needs, but that's just the way I am," you've identified the problem.

If there is any one personality trait that exemplifies the flesh, it is *selfishness*. All of the flesh's systems are designed for self-protection and self-preservation. Therefore self-centeredness is always a sign that the flesh is at work.

The next step in spotting these below-the-surface bondages is recognizing the subconscious pressures from external forces that affect you. Advertising is one of the most powerful. Even though you may "tune out" all the billboards and radio and TV ads, the messages are still being absorbed in your subconscious. You may have a tough time understanding how this works, but advertisers don't have any problem getting it. They spend a great deal of energy designing ads to send you subconscious signals about why you need to buy their products.

That's what happened to Alex in our example above. He never realized what was happening to him, or why, but the images he saw and the strip joint he passed resulted in subtle hormonal stimulation that caused sexual arousal—however slight—and subconscious sexual tension. When he took this tension home to his wife, it resulted in relational problems because she felt fleshly pressure—not love—motivating his affections.

These effects may be strongest on teenagers, whose hormones are already heightened, subjecting them to additional pressure. As young people take this subconscious pressure into dating situations, it can make choosing abstinence before marriage more of a struggle. Being aware of these stimuli and reducing them where possible can help limit the control your flesh has over your behavior.

Another example of subconscious fleshly influence is the impact advertising has on you. If you feel like you have to wear certain brand of clothing or drive a certain car to be happy, you likely have been convinced of that by subconscious messages in the ads around you. The advertisements may also come from the endorsements of friends around you who have already fallen captive to the subconscious mind game. The subtle, unspoken peer pressure you feel from those friends is another example of subconscious factors affecting you.

There is another telltale signal that will help you notice when subconscious fleshly mechanisms are at work in you: a deep sense of pressure. We talked about this fleshly pressure in chapter five when we discussed drivenness. It's a dead giveaway. Have you ever felt some feverish pressure urging you to behave in a certain way? If so, that's the clue you can use to know that you're being controlled by your flesh on a subconscious level. It is this deep sense of pressure that is telling you that your flesh is driving you in the wrong direction.

An example of how the subconscious pressures us and affects our actions without us consciously knowing it was seen when my sons were arguing recently. They were vehemently attacking one another over trivial matters. For a few days one angry response followed another, until my wife and I sat them down to find out what was going on.

At first neither really knew. All they knew was that they were upset with each other. A little probing revealed the younger brother was upset at feeling left out recently. The two were close in age and good friends who did almost everything together, until recently when a certain attractive young woman started taking more of the older brother's time.

The younger didn't know it, but his subconscious mind was keeping track of the amount of time his brother spent with him. The result of the analysis of this trend was that something was wrong. It hadn't quite reached his conscious understanding yet, but the negative subconscious feelings were definitely affecting his actions.

The same can happen in your life as different subconscious brain centers pressure you to respond in various ways. This inner pressure can produce the inner turmoil and out-of-control feelings that I previously described as the symptoms that occur when the flesh is in control. Now you see why these sensations are so deep and confusing. They are arising in your subconscious and working their way slowly to the surface.

Recognizing this subconscious pressure can help you in times when you're not quite sure what is right and what is wrong. If you feel driven or pressured toward some action or decision, it is flesh. The Spirit gently leads as a shepherd. He never pushes. The flesh, on the other hand, is a wild animal wanting only to dominate. You can easily sense the difference between the two now that you are learning the characteristics of the flesh.

Don't forget to listen as God tells you what issues you have with Him at the bottom of it all. There could be all types of disappointment with God leading to fleshly pressure affecting you subconsciously. This is where the major "You gypped me, God!" attitude affects your other responses. Getting down to the God issues here is going to require coming to grips with the fact that God made you the way He wants you, and He loves you like a Father and has only your best in mind. It may take some struggling with these attitudes to fully hear where you may be hung up subconsciously.

Admit

More than one teenager has told me, "Those R-rated movies don't affect me. I'm too mature for that. What do you think—if we watch movies we're going to run out and have sex?" Statements that minimize the impact of subconscious forces are the excuses that will keep you from fully admitting that you have a problem.

If you keep making excuses, more and more problems will work their way to the surface to convince you of the corruption below. Better to admit it now and get on with fixing the problem.

Submit

The submission stage is going to look a little different with subconscious fleshly influences than with others because you cannot very well choose to submit something you may not be aware of consciously. So if you are experiencing significant struggles and it feels like it is bubbling up from somewhere deep inside, I want you to first pray and submit your problem to God as one of those problems that you cannot submit. That will begin the process of regeneration using His supernatural healing power.

If you continue to struggle and your life is being undermined by thought processes and moods that just don't seem to have a recognizable source, I want you to consider submitting to a medical examination by your doctor. Surprised? Well, At this point in your struggle with the flesh you need to consider that there may be something physically wrong in you that can be helped by physical means. We have already discussed numerous physical processes that can cause problems if they were to malfunction.

Psychiatric illness presents a host of other disorders that can produce struggles. When dealing with psychiatric illness in the Christian setting, some take the purely spiritual view that all emotional problems result from spiritual problems and need to be dealt with spiritually. Others take the purely secular view that emotional illness is caused by physical or chemical imbalances that need to be corrected with medication.

Suffice it to say that neither of these statements is universally true. Taking an extreme position could result in casting out "demons of confusion" from a person with Alzheimer's disease, or giving antidepressants to someone who needs to deal with sin in her life. Both, of course, would be wrong. The truth lies in the understanding that we are both physical and spiritual and that both aspects need to be addressed.

After the birth of our first child, I had a conversation with my mother. It was time to get our daughter vaccinated, and my wife and I wrestled a bit with this decision since some Christians we had encountered felt it showed a lack of faith to vaccinate your children. And we wanted sincerely to be people of faith.

My mother said that when she was a child, everyone knew families that had been touched by polio. It was common to have children die or become crippled as a result of this disease that preyed on the young ones. As a result, she told me, parents all over cried out to God for a cure. By the time my mother was ready to have children of her own, a vaccination was available, and she thanked God for His divine answer to all of those prayers that came through the hands of researchers in the field of medicine.

Well, I was convinced. God can work through people, even if they are doctors. How stubborn of us to tell God He can only work in our lives supernaturally and not through natural, medical means if He chooses to.

Prudent use of antianxiety medications may be a significant help to calm the flesh and give you some rest in your mind to refocus your thoughts on God's Word while you continue in the sanctification process. A good night's sleep, aided by sleeping medication, may be just what you need to reenter the battle with your flesh. Antidepressants may stabilize your mood, reduce the influence of your emotions, and help you deal with problems more effectively.

In general, medication should be taken very judiciously and as a way to support, not avoid, the sanctification process. It should also be used for a precise medical reason and only under the supervision of a physician.

Trust

The key is to not look to the medical field for salvation. Christ is still your Savior, and ultimately you are relying on Him. If there is no clear evidence of an underlying physical problem, avoid medication. Remember that God uses struggles in your life to bring about your sanctification. If you relieve that struggling with medication, you may end up doing yourself more harm than good.

Consider a person who has her hand resting on a hot stove with the heat steadily increasing. She asks you what she should do to relieve the discomfort. If you offer her pain medication and she keeps her hand on the hot stove, you do her a disservice. She will suffer more damage in the long run than if you simply let the discomfort tell her that she needs to change her behavior and move her hand.

And remember: every time you avoid dealing with God on your issue, you schedule yourself for one more lap in the wilderness. So even if you use medical treatment to help in the process, make sure you are trusting in God to cleanse you of the subconscious problems in your flesh that need sanctification.

Stand firm

While you are standing firm—and praying and worshiping and seeking God—remember that it isn't just your *physical* senses that can be overloaded. Your *spiritual* senses can get blasted out, too. Just as it's hard to hear the voice of a friend in a loud room, so it's hard to hear the quiet voice of God when you're overwhelmed with other input.

One reason a blind person has a better sense of hearing is simply that he is not spending any energy concentrating on what he is seeing. A sighted person, conversely, will not hear as well as a blind person because he is distracted by the visual stimuli that dominate his attention.

In the same way, when we are being bombarded by stimuli from our physical senses, it is very difficult to receive information through our spiritual senses. We describe God as having a still, small voice. It's not that His voice is weak—it's our hearing that's bad. The effects of sin have left our spiritual senses feeble. Our spiritual sight was described by Paul as seeing "in a mirror dimly" (1 Corinthians 13:12) because our spiritual sense of sight is poor. Because of this, any distraction has a greater detrimental effect to our spiritual receptiveness.

To boost our ailing spiritual senses, we need to remove as many of the overpowering physical stimuli as we can in order to hear from God spiritually. When Jesus talked about going into your inner room and shutting the door to pray (Matthew 6:6), one of His reasons was so that external distractions would be eliminated. When we close the door, close our eyes, fold our hands—maybe even plug our ears—we are reducing distracting sounds, sights, and touch sensations, allowing us to focus our attention on receiving input from the Spirit.

Do you really need to hear from God right now? Are you facing a major decision and need His counsel? Then turn off the fleshly stimuli around you. Limit your time with worldly friends, turn off secular music and movies, unplug the television set, and eliminate anything else that creates fleshly stimuli that can distract you from the spiritual.

CHAPTER 9

EMOTIONS—THE CHEMISTRY BEHIND YOUR FEELINGS

WENDY

It's not that they're poor. They are far from that. It's just that things have been getting steadily tighter since Stan left his job for full-time ministry. Back then Wendy had sensed her husband's call and had even accepted the move out of state, but the pay cut is really starting to make things tough. And the promise that "God will provide" just isn't as comforting now as it had been when they started three years ago.

Today Stan walks through the door with that look. Wendy has gotten to know it all too well these past few years. It was the look that said, "Honey, I've got bad news." Apparently the meeting with the treasurer hadn't gone well. The ministry's funds were low.

Wendy knows a pay cut is coming even before Stan starts into the explanation. She looks away as he speaks. She's feeling trapped again. *There goes any thought of a vacation. And I was so ready to escape from this place for a little while.*

Stan tells her about the treasurer's report, but it only makes it worse. All she really hears is that there is no financial solution in sight to the ministry's cash flow problems.

That means we'll never be able to afford a home. And what about college for the kids someday?

Wendy's pulse quickens. She bites her lip to keep it from quivering. Stan talks about the great things God is doing in people's lives through his ministry and how he's thinking of taking a part-time job to see that the work continues.

And what if the ministry folds financially and I am stuck in this town with no friends, no ministry, and only a part-time job? How will we live then? Where will we go? What will we do?

Wendy can't listen anymore. She wants to ask the questions running through her mind, but she knows Stan doesn't have any answers. His upturned palms and the shrug of the shoulders confirm this. He looks understandingly into her eyes, eyes that now overflow in quiet tears.

Maybe Stan was all wrong with this calling thing. Maybe we should have just stayed where we were.

She leaves the room to wrap in an afghan and curl into her favorite chair by the bay window. The one thing she likes about living here is the view. But this time she can't even enjoy that. She gazes out of the window with her mind swimming with tormenting thoughts. The words that finally send her from the room are the ones she now hates to hear: "We just have to trust God."

Ha! Trust God. Where has that gotten us?

AL

There are toddler toys just inside the door again. Again! Al kicks a scooter out of the way, smashing it against the far wall, and slams the door.

"Theresa! How many times have I told you that I want the kids' things out of the doorway so I don't have to trip over them when I get home from work? And why are you holding my daughter behind your back like that? You think I'm some kind of wild animal or something? That's stupid."

"Well, honey," she says in that sniveling voice, "you know the kids like it because the toys roll better on the tile. I was just coming to pick them up."

"Sure you were." He watches as she finally picks up some of the clutter. What does she do all day?

"Bad day at work?"

"Of course I had a bad day!" Al bellows. "Boy, does that Rick know how to push my buttons. He knows just how to make me look stupid in front of the boss." Al pulls at the zipper on his coat, nearly tearing it off. "And it would help if

Emotions—The Chemistry Behind Your Feelings

I didn't have to kick my way into the house!"

"Certainly, honey," she says, still holding little Marie to herself. "Maybe you could calm down now, though."

Al grits his teeth and exhales hard, nearly growling. "Calm down! Yeah, I'll calm down—when I'm good and ready."

He tosses down his coat and stomps into the living room. Someone's at the TV already. It's their son, watching some worthless cartoon. With a quick grab Al reaches down to jerk his son to his feet with a fistful of shirt.

"And you—haven't I told you to finish your homework before you sit in front of the boob tube?"

The kid stands nearly at attention. "Yes, sir."

What am I, a drill sergeant?

"But I only have a little, Daddy. I thought I'd do it after dinner."

"Well, why don't you think again and go do it now?" Al shoves him toward the stairs, sending him stumbling and tripping as he runs for his bedroom. "And don't you whine at me, boy. You sound like your mother."

Al drops into his recliner and reaches for the remote. Ah, the blessed remote. The ultimate symbol of mastery. Here, in his throne, with his scepter of power, he rules all he surveys. So what if he sends the rest of his family cowering into other parts of the house?

Don't Get All Emotional on Me

Wendy and Al seem very different, don't they? But they have at least one thing in common: they are both ruled by their emotions. Wendy nurses her feelings of fear, and Al feeds his feelings of frustration to the point that he has become a terror to his own family.

Emotions are one of the most powerful and complex aspects of the human flesh. Did you catch that? I said that *emotions*, which many people consider to be entirely nonphysical, are part of the flesh. As we will see, emotions clearly are rooted in the physical processes of our bodies.

Many people see emotions as the opposite, even the opponent, of rational thought. In reality, emotions are produced by the same processes that produce drives, defensiveness, and all the other fleshly symptoms we've looked at. Namely, emotions rely on our old friends, the neurological pathways.

While we like to think of emotions as being "the way we feel," they really are the result of a series of complex neurologic signals that combine to give us that feeling. Within the limbic system, which we introduced in the last chapter, there are groups of nerve cells that are specially designed to produce an emotional response.

You may consider yourself a rather unemotional person, but unless your limbic system has failed entirely, that simply can't be true. Nearly every sensory input and output response pathway has a connection in the limbic system. What that means is that every time your brain receives a stimulus from an incoming sensory pathway—what someone says, the sight of certain person, a familiar smell, etc.—the signal is sent through the limbic system. Why? So it can be analyzed for its emotional content. This helps you understand what the sensory input means to you so you can form an appropriate response.

It can be the very subtle analysis of the tones people use in conversation. If someone says, "Well, that's just *great!*" you get ready to celebrate with him. If he says, "Well, that's *just* great," you detect the sarcasm and get ready to deal with a problem. The same words are received, but a different emotional response is chosen.

In short, your emotional system enhances nearly every one of your brain's responses in some way. This trip through the limbic system is part of the *analysis* step in the neurologic pathway (stimulus received, stimulus analyzed, response generated). That's important. The emotions are not ends, in and of themselves—they're part of how your brain decides upon a proper response. Emotions are there simply to help us better understand the significance of an incoming signal.

When the limbic system has figured out the emotional content of the input, that information is added into the mix. It's taken into consideration along with all the other analysis done during step two of the neurologic pathway, and finally a response is chosen.

Remember how your body interpreted the back rub in the previous chapter? Well, as the sensory information regarding touch is analyzed, your limbic system is going to help you decide whether the pain and pressure you are feeling are good things or bad things.

It evaluates the signals for their precise characteristics, and then it determines that these sensations are not intended to cause damage but rather pleasure. So the limbic system enhances the signal with a pleasurable response, and you say, "*Ahhhh.*"

Have you ever suddenly jerked away and yelled "Ouch!" during a deep muscle massage? Well, that was your limbic system drawing the line and saying that now the masseuse has crossed over from therapy to threat. Instead of signaling a pleasurable emotion, the limbic system realizes it's time to sound an alarm, and the stress response pathways of the brain are activated.

"OK," you may be saying, "maybe touch sensations can be interpreted emotionally, but can emotions as complex as love, hate, or fear really be based on neurologic signals?"

The answer is most definitely *yes*. Just as you can make the arm jump by electrically stimulating the part of the brain that controls the muscles of the arm, so you can artificially stimulate the limbic system to produce an emotion. Experiments have shown that if you place an electrode into the appropriate area of the limbic system in a lab animal and stimulate it, the animal will express a rage response: hissing, growling, and showing claws and teeth. Stimulating other areas will result in the animal becoming docile, showing fear, or displaying pleasure.

It stands to reason that our emotions too are not entirely esoteric or spiritual, but they are firmly rooted in the physical.

That's hard to accept, isn't it? How can our own highest feelings—love, joy, peace—be the result of something so base as cells and neurons? The reason it is difficult to believe is that emotions are complex. An emotion is not just a single response, such as moving a muscle. Creating an emotion requires many responses throughout the body combining to give you the final feeling that you identify as a particular emotion.

If you are alone in an unfamiliar place, for instance, and you suddenly hear a loud crash in another part of the building, your limbic system goes to work sending signals all throughout your nervous system. Your conscious mind starts thinking about the possibility of murderers and thieves approaching. A quick signal is sent to your stress centers so your heart starts pounding and your breathing quickens. Another response signal goes to the little muscles attached to the hair follicles on your arms so that you get "goose bumps" and your "skin crawls." The result: an emotion of fear.

Other emotions are similar. Keep the pounding heart and rapid breathing, but change the thoughts from fear to hopes of life-long companionship. Add the dilation of skin blood vessels to give you a warm flush, and now you are feeling in love.

Emotions are wonderfully complex and tremendously good at producing strong effects on our lives. They play an important role in helping us to live our lives in this fleshly world. They are, after all, one of the good things God created. But our emotions are thoroughly rooted in our flesh, as we have seen.

Hormones

As if the neurologic pathways involved in emotions were not complicated enough, there is another factor adding to their complexity: hormones.

It's no secret that hormones affect our emotions. Ask any woman, and she'll tell you that hormones can have a dramatic effect on your emotional state. The emotional swings related to menstruation are due to the female sex hormones estrogen and progesterone. As their concentrations vary in the bloodstream over the course of a month, a woman's emotions will vary with them. The result is sometimes mood changes that can be quite severe. This can produce all types of strain on relationships. And, since my wife is going to read this, I think I'll just leave this discussion right here!

But men shouldn't think it is only women whose behavior is affected by hormones. Men have swings in their testosterone levels, too. In a way, they may actually be worse because they're far less predictable. If you don't believe me, just observe teenage boys when a pretty girl enters the room. Their muscles tighten, their posture changes, their walk takes on a little swagger, and their voice gets a little stronger. Suddenly the guys are pushing and shoving and acting tough. There's nothing like a little testosterone surge!

And there is no doubt that it's fleshly. It's downright animalistic. If the same girl would put her mind to it, she could even get the boys to start butting heads together like deer in heat. And honestly, it isn't just teenagers. Hang around anyplace where single men congregate, inject an attractive woman into the mix, and the result is the same.

Sex hormones are not the only ones that cause mood shifts. Imbalances of thyroid hormone are one of the most common hormonal causes of emotional problems. And I've already mentioned the powerful responses produced by adrenaline during stress. Prolonged stimulation by adrenaline is known to produce mood swings, anxiety, and fatigue.

Another group of stress hormones, the corticosteroids, can also cause mood changes up and down, and in extreme cases even psychosis. Medical supplementation with corticosteroids can cause feelings of euphoria. Prolonged corticosteroid stimulation in stress can cause anxiety and fatigue similar to that caused by adrenaline.

Dopamine and serotonin are two important chemicals that are related to hormones like those mentioned above. As we said previously, they are neurotransmitters, chemicals that nerve cells use to communicate with each other. While their activities are only partly understood, they are known to play a significant role in emotions. Many "emotional problems"—depressive disorders and other psychiatric illnesses—are attributed to imbalances in these neurotransmitters. A number of commonly prescribed psychiatric medications adjust the concentration or function of these hormones in order to help stabilize the person's emotional disorder.

Many more hormones affect the way our bodies function and thus contribute to our emotional state. The brief descriptions above only scratch the surface of the complex neurologic and hormonal systems that affect our emotions. It does show, however, how dependent our emotions are on our physical systems. They are utterly fleshly and, therefore, must come under the control of the Spirit.

Emotions in Charge

While emotions add wonderful texture and strength to our lives, they can also produce problems. Your legs are great devices, too, but if you break one, you won't walk so well. The same is true when illness or injury in the limbic system causes disruption of the neurologic pathways. In this case, your emotions don't work so well. This can cause wrong or exaggerated emotional responses to stimuli.

If the hormones that affect our feelings rise or drop in their levels, that's a chemical imbalance, and it is just as physical as when a diabetic has abnormal insulin levels. So, it is important to not dump emotional issues into a separate category and treat them differently. They need to be dealt with the same way we deal with other problems in the flesh. This includes a diligent pursuit of sanctification of the flesh, which at times may include getting some medical help if there is an abnormality with the way your body handles emotions.

Even with all the right physical processes in place, however, your fleshly emotions can still take control and mess things up. And dealing with a limbic system that's out of whack is quite a bit different from just taking a shot of insulin when your blood sugar rises. Hopefully now you can see why—the limbic system is literally wired into almost every other part of your nervous system. So, there is a lot of potential for crossed wires. If you were hoping to just pop a Prozac and have your struggling disappear—sorry, it's probably not going to be that easy.

The good news is that since your limbic system is wired into so many other places, there are a lot of ways you can affect your emotions. So, let's start looking at ways to deal with them.

Treatment Plan

Listen

Finding emotions is never a problem. You wake up in the morning with a smile, and your limbic system says, "What a great day!" You get to work, and your boss yells at you. Now your limbic system says, "Man, does this day stink." Your emotions are there all the time responding to the stimuli you receive. And that's not a problem. In fact, it is a good thing. It helps you understand the significance of the different stimuli you encounter.

In the interaction with the boss above, what your limbic system is really saying is, "Hey, the boss is mad. This needs to be dealt with seriously." And that little emotional signal is going to help you give the appropriate response to your boss.

It's the inappropriate emotional responses that we are looking for when trying to identify problem areas in the flesh. One way to spot them is to look for *repetitive emotions*. They're the ones you keep having over and over. Since emotions are the result of neurologic processes, they will have predictable outcomes. When the same stimulus comes, you fire the same neurologic pathway, resulting in the same emotional response.

It is just like the signals that move your arm. When you fire up the nerves to your arm, your arm moves every time. The only difference is that these neurologic signals are not designed to produce movement or a change in organ function. They produce a feeling.

Most of us have experienced the reality of how predictable this physical process can be. We all know people who seem to know exactly what to do or say to make us mad, frustrated, or feeling guilty. There are also people who know just the right thing to say to cheer us up.

We often say these people "know how to push our buttons." And really, this description is accurate because the response that is generated from the stimulus is as predictable as pushing a button on a machine. What they are doing is giving you the right stimulus to activate the appropriate neurologic pathway that leads to the emotional response they want to produce in you. It's like you're a vending machine.

In our example, Al recognized that Rick was repeatedly stimulating his emotions. Unfortunately, he didn't deal with Rick or his own "emotional buttons." Instead, he let his emotions take control and make him—not to mention his family—miserable.

If you have a button that gets pushed over and over, you have found an area of fleshly emotion that needs to be dealt with.

Another signal that the flesh is controlling your emotions is when you have *exaggerated emotions*. Your emotions were designed to add emphasis in the analysis phase to help you respond to situations. If their response is out of proportion to the problem, this overshadows the original issue, and the emotions become a problem themselves. Al is a good example. The anger he showed with the kids' toys and the kids themselves was way overboard. He may not have known it, but it was a signal that he has a deeper problem.

Let's look at a less drastic emotional response as an example. Suppose you and your spouse run into your high school sweetheart on the street one day. During the analysis step, in which your brain is trying to figure out how to respond, your limbic system says, "Hey, pay attention to this. This person is different from others. I'm going to give you a little different feeling so you will give this encounter a little more attention and a different type of response." You then develop a response that has the right *feeling*. You give your old flame a hug—enough to say you're a friend and nothing more—and you part ways. An appropriate response is given, and afterward, the emotion goes away and life is back to normal.

That's the way emotions are designed to work. What you want to look for in the listening phase are times when your emotions take over and cause you to blow it in certain situations.

Another way an emotion can be exaggerated is when it affects you after a response has been given. Let's go back to the old flame encounter. Suppose you allow the emotions to linger, and you think, "Wow, it was really great seeing that special person again. Boy, the fun we had. Ah, the memories..." Suddenly you're enjoying the rush of emotion produced by the encounter. The emotional stimulus that was designed to alert you to the importance of a significant stimulus is now taking center stage and creating a situation of its own.

Enjoying this little walk down memory lane is not such a problem, but it is of the flesh, and it does give the flesh a little foothold. Suppose after enjoying those memories you go home and start really dwelling on those old feelings. Maybe next you are creating new emotions by fantasizing about what life would be like if you had stayed together. If the flesh's exaggerated responses go unchecked, you are in for trouble.

Keep in mind here that in our example there is no situation that needs an emotional response any longer. You're married, so there is no need to think about any kind of relationship with this person. If the thoughts aren't going away, it's because you're not letting them. You're basking in the feeling of it. Keep it up, and your spouse will throw a little something your way to help you identify that this has become a problem!

Another way your emotions can take over is with *emotional miscalculation*. This is when your limbic system miscalculates things and sends off a flare when there is no real emergency. Let's face it; it's possible to just plain mess up while going through the analysis step of the process and thus end up producing a wrong response.

My daughter, a competitive cheerleader in senior high school, demonstrated emotional miscalculation wonderfully one year while the team was preparing for competition. They had come in second in the state the previous year, and now they were working very hard to be number one. A few weeks before the competition, she came home from practice in tears, and she stayed upset for days. Why? A key member of the team had gotten hurt. It seemed there was no way to adjust their routine at so late a date. She was distraught. Her limbic system was telling her there was no hope.

We would later find out that her limbic system had gotten it all wrong—they won the state championship. So what were all the anguish and tears for? Nothing. It was all due to a miscalculation somewhere in the process that produced her emotions.

You need to be very suspicious of your own emotional responses. Don't let them overshadow the situation they are alerting you to, because then they can become a problem themselves.

Again, emotions are not bad. They just need to stay under control, like every other part of the flesh. In my daughter's case, the feelings of concern actually helped everyone on the team focus and work a little harder, so that when crunch time came, they were ready. To let their emotions take over, however, could have weakened the team members with despair.

As you ask God to show you where your flesh is in control, keep an eye out for emotional responses that take over and become a situation themselves rather than helping you respond to a particular situation. When you find this happening, start looking for the deeper layers of problems that might be triggering these wrong feelings. And don't forget to keep digging until you reach your beef with God that is making you so emotional.

Admit

Identifying emotions may not be tough, but admitting they are a problem sure is. The reason is because they are so personal. Since our emotions are tools designed to identify the importance of situations, they define what is important to us. If we have a strong emotion over something, it means it's significant and we want others to see it as important, too.

That's why it's really tough to have someone tell you, "Oh, don't get so upset; it's not that important." What they are really saying is that it is not important to them and it shouldn't be to you. But it is—because your limbic system said it is.

So you have to be willing to be a little vulnerable. You have to lay down the defenses. And most of all you are going to have to come to grips with the reality that even though your limbic system is telling you there is a crisis, you really may just be exaggerating the situation. You may need to admit you are wrong.

What you are admitting is not that you have emotions, or that having them is wrong. You are allowed to be angry, happy, frustrated, excited, depressed, overjoyed, and all the rest. That's how God designed you. What you have to admit is when those emotions are controlling you and creating problems of their own.

Usually that is what your helpful friends really want to say when they tell you to not be so upset. They are helping you identify where your emotions have gotten out of control. That's the time you have to admit that the flesh is taking over and that you need a change.

Submit

Then it is time for a choice. You can't choose what emotion your limbic system is going to attach to any particular stimulus. But there is an important choice you can make. This is the choice to not do something I call *emotional recycling*.

Recycling takes place when the response from the limbic system reaches your conscious mind and alerts you to the importance of something—"That's my high school sweetheart"—and then you send the signal *back* to the limbic system to reactivate a fresh surge of emotions—"Oh, but it was good to see that person again!" So you get another little surge. And again—"Boy, the fun we had."

Bigger surge. And again—"Ah, the memories." *Kaboom* surge.

Sending it back to the limbic system? Do you have some strange neurologic disorder that causes your brain pathways to flow backward? No. Emotional recycling is something you choose to do with the emotional stimuli that affect you. "I liked how I felt when I saw my old flame. And when I think about it now, I like it even more."

Starting to sound familiar? Your flesh craves sensation, remember? It grooves on pleasurable sensory input. It even likes the bad sensations. Sure, they hurt, they're sad, they're angry—many of the emotions that control us are the negative ones—but still it wants more of it.

To keep those emotional sensations alive, you focus on a thought that becomes a new stimulus to start the cycle back through the neurologic pathways again. Every time you recycle the emotion, you get another emotional "buzz" from the fleshly impulses. Just like the other sensations we talked about, the more times you feel a sensation, the more your body down-regulates the pathway, and you need more and more. And you're hooked! You gave your fleshly emotions control, and now you are in bondage to them.

One of the most commonly recycled feelings is the feeling of hurt. You may know in your spirit that forgiveness is the way to freedom, but it just feels too good to stay hurt. A feeling of hurt comes along, and your flesh cries, "Oh, how he hurt me," sending a surge of emotion with it. The Spirit urges you to forgive, and you may even consider it a moment, but then you decide to send a new surge through your limbic system with, "Oh, but he *really* hurt me." Choosing to recycle the emotion is a critical decision that gives the flesh control and results in bondage.

Notice that it is you, not the person who hurt you, who is now adding to the pain of the situation by recycling. You're blaming the other person for the hurt, but you're doing the add-on hurting yourself. It's like someone knocked you down, so now you keep knocking yourself down over and over to remind yourself of how bad it hurt. It reminds me of the scene in *Liar, Liar* when Jim Carrey beats the tar out of himself in the men's room. The other person caused the first stimulus that triggered the first wave of emotion, but you have caused the rest.

Look at worrying Wendy's responses. The problem that she and her husband face is real, and her initial feelings of concern are alerting her there is a problem that is going to need some serious attention. Her emotional responses are also a signal to her husband that she needs some extra help during this difficult time.

But as that signal reaches its conclusion, Wendy takes it one step further, and then another and another. She hovers over the fear, feeding it and nourishing it until it grows ever stronger. She takes the problem facing her at the moment and adds to it one problem after another—none of which may ever turn into an actual problem in the future.

What she is doing is sending a new signal back to her limbic system to re-stimulate a fresh round of emotional responses again and again. She is recycling her emotional stimuli to get another burst of sensation. And her flesh loves it. It is basking in the stimulation. And every time the emotions are recycled, they grow in intensity and gain power over her—and you and me.

Eventually the emotional response becomes an issue itself, and Wendy becomes consumed with fear. This crippling fear may even come to overshadow the original problem in severity. By recycling her emotions Wendy is making herself worry about vacations, house payments, and paying for the kids' college, when all she really has to deal with right now is her husband's current ministry position.

If she could clear her head of the swirling emotions, she and Stan could seek the Lord and find His answer. Maybe He wants them to make a change. Maybe He wants them to stay where they are and learn to trust Him as they see all their needs met. But she will never find the answer while her fleshly emotions are controlling her.

Next time you find yourself in a situation with escalating emotions, stop and examine yourself to see if you're recycling. Try to identify when you are choosing to send the feelings back around for one more cycle of emotion. Are you choosing to dwell on something and getting more and more upset? It may be feelings of fear as with Wendy, or hurt, anger, frustration, or any other emotion. If you are, it is time to break the cycle and choose to stop adding thoughts that re-stimulate your emotions.

Trust

While it sounds good to identify where your emotions are exaggerated, repetitive, miscalculated, or being recycled, it is harder than you may think. Remember that these neurologic pathways travel as electrical signals, so they happen pretty fast. Your time of decision may be only a split second and happen in between words just as a wrong response is leaving your mouth.

For you to have any chance at all in making the right choice in these brief moments, you are going to need a work of God to slow things down and weaken your fleshly emotions so that they don't respond so quickly or so strongly.

When you recognize that your emotional state is an uncontrolled "fleshfest," it is time to call out to God for help. You've confessed the flesh's control of your life as sin; now trust Him to cleanse you of it.

Stand firm

Even as God does a work in your life, it is going to take some time to break the power that fleshly emotions hold over you. Initially you may only recognize the problem after it has escalated and caused a disaster. That's the time to say, "Hey, that argument was my emotions getting out of control. I'm sorry. I'm working on that."

Stand firm. Don't give up on the process.

Eventually you'll be able to spot the emotions as they begin to escalate. Perhaps you'll recycle the feeling a few times but then catch yourself. Then you can say, "Wait, this is crazy. Let's back up and just deal with the problem."

Keep standing firm.

Finally, you'll feel the temptation to dwell on some feeling—and you'll be able to not give in at all. Your standing firm will have turned to victory, and you will have brought the power of your fleshly emotions under the control of the Spirit.

CHAPTER 10

INTERNAL REWARDS—YOUR NEUROLOGIC MOTIVES

MICHELLE

Everybody says that Michelle is the godliest young woman in the church. Mothers half-jokingly ask her if she'll wait a few years to get married so their sons can grow up and snag her. She's grounded in her Bible, gifted in service, and uncontainable in worship. Speculation has it that she'll either go into full-time ministry or stay here and be the first female deacon in their church's history.

As for Michelle herself, she likes to discount the praise people give her. She appears uncomfortable and urges folks to praise God instead. But she does have to admit to a nice little warm glow that comes when people say things like that. In fact, she says it's part of why she enjoys ministry. She feels it when the kids in Sunday school sit rapt before her teaching—and when their parents praise her afterward. She feels it when she's reluctantly prevailed upon to get up to the microphone to make announcements some Sunday mornings. And she definitely feels it when she lifts her arms in worship. Sometimes she even drops to her knees, so engrossed in worship she becomes.

"Why would anyone want to pursue sin when serving the Lord is so gratifying?" Michelle often wonders. "I guess they just don't have the same level of sincere commitment."

Say Goodbye to Stubborn Sin

Nick

Nick grabs his gear and starts methodically preparing for the day's mission. They still aren't sure if chemical weapons are going to be used against them, so today they are at MOPP 1 (Mission-Oriented Protective Posture, Level One) with their chemical warfare gear in place and ready. Nick puts on his CPU (chemical protective undergarment) and J-list suit over it. He stashes his gloves and boot and helmet covers and straps his mask to his left thigh. Finally he drops his helmet on his head, swings his Kevlar vest over one arm, shoulders his M-16, and trots out to his vehicle.

Nick climbs into one of the two Humvees that is carrying his squad and pops his head up through the turret to begin preparing the .50 caliber weapon he mans. They are soon joined by the other Hummers and Bradley fighting vehicles that carry the rest of their light infantry platoon. The last minor tasks of fastening the clasps on his vest and securing his ammunition allow for a few moments to consider the horrors of war that might await him in the next few hours. He knows other American units have already lost lives, and the assault on Baghdad has only just begun. A picture of his wife and kids floats through his mind along with a silent prayer.

The sound of his lieutenant's voice rouses him from thought. "Listen here, men. Today a dictator who has killed thousands of his own people and supported terrorism against the United States of America is going to fall." His voice rises in intensity, slowing down to emphasize each word of *United States of America*. "Look at the man on your right and on your left, and remember when you get into battle that's who you're fighting for—and every man comes home!"

Nick nods his head and reflects on the Marine code.

"The president has given us a job to do," the lieutenant says. He pauses to allow the words to sink in. "Now, let's go do it!"

Nick's heart is swelling and ready to burst. And finally it does as the emotion erupts out of him and he joins with his platoon in a cheer of "Oooraah!"

His images of home are stowed away with all of his other gear. Now he is a soldier entering battle. He throws the

Internal Rewards—Your Neurologic Motives

bolt on his .50 caliber to advance the ammunition belt and chamber a new round of ammunition. His sights are set on the city ahead.

Let's go topple us a dictator.

Neurologic Doggy Treats

Michelle sounds like a pretty decent girl, doesn't she? And really she is. She's a great girl and a good Christian, but she's still human. And as a human she is subject to all of the limitations of the flesh, which, as we have seen, can be rather twisted and complicated.

So, what's wrong with her? Why do I have her as an example for the chapter? Remember Steve in chapter five, who volunteered in church because it was his conditioned response—which he later regretted? Well, as I promised, we are going to revisit our hidden motives and find another area of our flesh that makes us do the right things for the wrong reasons.

This one is a little different, though. With this area there are no regrets. You won't find Michelle later saying she wished she wasn't such a good Christian. No way. This one feels good all the way through, which is one of the reasons why it is so powerful and so dangerous. It is also powerful because it can be turned around and cause good sensations for bad responses, like resentment and bitterness. It is the reason we love to hold on to these attitudes, even as they are destroying us.

I'm talking about another part of your body, something called the *system of internal rewards*. Deep inside the brain lie neurologic pathways that generate a wide array of deep, pleasurable sensations that act as positive reinforcement to the activities that occurred just before their stimulation.

Experiments performed using rats with electrodes implanted within this system in the brain demonstrated its effects.[1] When the electrodes were stimulated, rats would show the actions and body posturing associated with pleasurable activities. The rats enjoyed the stimulation so much that they could be directed around an open field by simply giving a brief stimulus when they looked in the direction the experimenter wanted them to go. They could also be directed through a complex maze using stimulation to this area of the brain as their only reward. They could literally be steered around by giving them the reward of a positive jolt of pleasurable neurologic signals when they behaved the way the researcher wanted.

This stimulation proved to be a very powerful reward. In other experiments, animals were willing to cross a painful, electrified grid to receive the stimulation. They were also willing to neglect feeding and sexual activity in preference of the internal stimulation.

And this same system exists in you and me. Though it's tough to find people willing to let you experiment on them by sticking electrodes in their brain, the same neurologic centers are present in our brains producing similar effects.

The positive rewards are basically a little neurologic "doggy treat" that you get for performing a good behavior. Do a good little action, and your neurologic pathways give you a nice little reward in response. These pathways intertwine areas of the brain from the brain stem all the way to the cerebrum and affect both conscious and subconscious centers. They are primarily centered in the limbic system and the frontal lobe of the cerebrum, the same areas associated with emotions.

Though they are linked to the limbic system, the responses of the internal rewards system are stronger and more far-reaching than our standard emotions. They are more closely associated with subconscious centers and therefore probably produce a deeper, more general sensation such as the strong, deep feelings associated with pride, satisfaction, honor, and similar feelings that follow some action. These sensations are very powerful feelings that direct our lives in significant ways. If we're not careful, they can direct us around just like rats.

How many times do we press on to the completion of a difficult task in order to feel the strong sense of well-being and satisfaction associated with the "sense of accomplishment" or to enjoy the feeling of a "a job well done"? I enjoyed these sensations a few summers ago when I made a little garden and planted a few fruit trees in our yard. For the next few days I would wander through the yard just to feel the sense of satisfaction that came following the project. These commonly understood sensations are part of the internal sensations that you get as a reward from your nervous system.

It could also be the feeling new parents have when they display their little treasure to friends while beaming with pride. It can be seen as the strong internal feelings that accompany a sense of honor that compels a soldier like Nick to go bravely into battle. Because of his feelings of loyalty to his brothers in arms, Nick locked away his normal good sense that would compel him to drive away from danger, and instead he ran to the guns. These are powerful forces. People will go to great lengths to obtain these feelings, and in the case of the soldier, even risking life itself.

These powerful, positive sensations can also be linked to less virtuous experiences. There is a strong sense of satisfaction that we experience when we watch an enemy suffer and be defeated. A strong feeling of superiority wells up deep from within us as we think about someone less attractive, less wealthy, or less intelligent than ourselves.

Motives

We may also enjoy deeply satisfying feelings of self-righteousness when we think of how our religious commitment or acts of service exceed those of others. In my example above, Michelle may be caught in this very trap. Her religious fervor may be out of a desire to receive a little burst of internal reward rather than sincere service to God.

Now don't get me wrong; this can be a good way that our flesh was designed to help us stay motivated for good behaviors. God's design for our flesh includes lots of things that help us live out our lives here in the flesh. But it is still flesh, and since it is flesh, it can be corrupted by sin. When it is, our motives can be fleshly.

Christ knew that this was a potential problem and warned us to guard against having fleshly rewards motivate our spiritual activities. In Matthew 6:1–5 He cautioned that those who do this will not be rewarded by their heavenly Father because they already have their reward in full. Part of this is, no doubt, the internal reward given by our nervous system.

How many spiritual activities do you and I participate in just because they make us feel good about ourselves deep inside? And if this is our motivation, does it really constitute a spiritual activity at all, or is it just a fleshly response? It's kind of a scary thought, isn't it?

When we do good things for others, for instance, is it because we really want to see them benefited, or is it to get a positive internal stimulus? Could philanthropy and generosity just be ways we produce these internal sensations? Have you ever heard someone describe the good feeling he got by helping someone else? There you have it—a little electric zap right from that electrode deep in the brain to guide you through the rat maze.

Could it be that it is better to give than to receive because giving stimulates the internal reward system and receiving does not?

Before you say, "No! Never! My motives are pure!" remember that rats were willing to give up eating and sex, and endure the pain of an electric grid, to get these very strong positive internal rewards. They had no idea what was motivating them when some scientist pushed a button and sent a signal through their brain. But when the internal reward system fired, they responded accordingly. They were completely oblivious to what was really motivating them to make the choices they did as they walked around the maze.

How about the maze of the world that you walk around in? Would you really know if a deeply subconscious sense from an internal reward was motivating the choices you make every day? Probably not.

The deep devotion to your spouse, your patriotism, and your religious fervor—much of it may be to experience the deep sense of satisfaction that your neurologic pathways are designed to give you. It would appear that even your best motives, the ones you thought were so purely spiritual, are also rooted in your flesh. It is not hard to understand why the Bible declares that "the heart is...desperately wicked; who can know it?" (Jeremiah 17:9, KJV). Even our best choices revolve around our self and our own pleasure, or our internal desire to maintain a state of well-being.

There is a negative reward, as well. This half of the internal reward system will give a deeply unpleasant sensation as a result of an action that is bad. This is probably where feelings like guilt and regret are generated. Although it is not the typical "reward" we would think of, there are negative sensations produced after some actions. The scientists could steer the rats away from the

INTERNAL REWARDS—YOUR NEUROLOGIC MOTIVES

direction they weren't to go by triggering these bad feelings. These internal stimuli were also very motivating.

What powerful portion of our lives does this sound like, something inside us that encourages good behavior and discourages bad behavior? How about the conscience? The conscience and the internal reward systems in the brain may be one and the same. Both use preprogrammed standards that God placed in our flesh to make us feel good or bad about what we do. As Paul describes, "...the Law written in their hearts, their conscience bearing witness and their thoughts alternately accusing or else defending them" (Romans 2:15).

You do something good, and *zap!* You feel good about it. You do something wrong, and *zing!* Not so good.

And this works pretty well, except for one little problem. Sin. When sin entered the picture, a few of your wires got crossed. Now things that are bad may not give you that bad feeling. Many a would-be sinner has fallen prey to the deceit of sin that says, "How could it be wrong if it feels so right?" Sin makes us lose the bad feeling that was supposed to accompany bad actions. The conscience has become seared (1 Timothy 4:2).

What's even worse is when bad responses feel good. Did you ever feel that deeply satisfying feeling that sometimes accompanies unforgiveness? You know what I mean—it occurs when you are hurt, and you deserve to be mad. The thought of the offense is painful, yet somehow deep inside you like it. No, you love it. And you love it so much that you hold on to it even as it destroys your relationships.

This is a frequent cause of struggling that causes a lot of confusion because you both love and hate the situation. Now you know why: there are two different fleshly systems at work. You might feel so angry and hate that emotion, but it stimulates the internal reward system, and you like that feeling. What a fleshly mess!

This also explains why feelings like hurt, resentment, unforgiveness, and bitterness are so strong—we like the way they make us feel. Not the emotion, but the internal reward we feel along with them. This makes removing these damaging feelings from our lives very difficult, because we know they are wrong, but we also like them and want to hold on to them.

You can recycle these sensations just as we said you could do with emotions. This really gives them power in your life. Every so often you just bring the memory of the original offense back to the surface so you can re-stimulate your system of internal rewards and feel these intense sensations again and again. We often refer to this as people "stewing in their juices" as they ruminate over past events, growing in anger and frustration over the horrible feelings, and loving every moment of it somewhere deep inside.

Gaining control of this area of the flesh means getting the good sensations linked back to the good actions and the bad to the bad. Let's start looking at getting this area of the flesh under the control of the Spirit.

Treatment Plan

Listen

Keep alert for those warm, pleasurable surges that seem to well up inside and make you glow all over. It probably wouldn't be so bad if you felt it while walking through your lush, fruitful garden enjoying a sense of accomplishment. But if you find yourself on stage in ministry, basking in the glow of your own limelight, watch out—you may not be quite as "spiritual" as you think.

This problem can be tough to spot since the outward actions are actually good. We've talked about that a number of times in this book, haven't we? I mean, look at Michelle—from all appearances she looks like a spiritual giant. The problem is that her flesh is motivating her, and by definition that means the ultimate results will be bad. Usually what happens in this situation is that the fleshly motives show themselves as soon as ministry is no longer fun or doesn't generate praises from people anymore. People hooked on the praise of others have to "feel called to another church" to find a place where the high level of praise hits can more easily be attained.

Do you enjoy the good feeling you get when involved in ministry? That's wonderful. I do, too. It's one of the rewards God gives us this side of heaven. However, while this good feeling can be a very good thing to keep you motivated, it can also become a snare. If you find yourself volunteering for ministry just to get that good feeling, or if you're irked when you don't get the credit

INTERNAL REWARDS—YOUR NEUROLOGIC MOTIVES

you feel you deserve, it may be that the flesh is in control.

You can also bask in the warm surges of bad feelings. In a strange way, negative feedback can be an addictive reward, too. You'd recognize this as times when you are stewing over painful situations. What you're really doing is enjoying positive internal rewards that are wrongly attached to bad responses. God's Word says that when you are resentful or unforgiving, it is a bad thing (Matthew 18:21–35). The problem is that sin has messed up your programming, and now you don't feel as bad about it as you should—in fact, you like it. It is very satisfying to feel so right that you are justified in hating someone else.

Start by recognizing that this is wrong and that if you are struggling, there is an issue in you that you need to deal with. Yes, the person who hurt you probably has issues, too, but you're much better off dealing with yours and letting God handle the rest of His unruly kids.

As you're looking for those positive rewards, keep an eye out for the negative ones as well. That's when bad feelings follow bad actions. Guilt is a bad feeling that follows a bad action, and it is a classic example of a negative reward. It's a good thing when it is keeping us in check and out of trouble, but many people are in bondage to guilt. Christ came to set us free from condemnation, not enslave us to bad feelings. A true, spiritual understanding of grace and forgiveness should free you from guilt. If you're not free, you may have given the flesh control of this area to the point that it's addicted to feeling guilty.

When you're in this condition, others can manipulate you through false guilt. They lay it on thick—stimulating a negative internal reward—to get you to do something they want you to do, or vice versa. This is a powerfully motivating tool to keep your head spinning and keep you in bondage. Again, if guilt is motivating you, there is something wrong.

Keep an ear out for the Spirit whispering to you as you consider whether these areas of your flesh are controlling you. And don't forget to dig all the way down to the God issue. In this area of the flesh you're going to have to burrow all the way down to your motives for serving Him. Is it because you love Him and are appreciative of the blessing of salvation, or just a cheap thrill?

Admit

Spotting the source of your motives is the tough part. Once you've identified your bad motives, it's not so hard to admit them. When God really opens your eyes, you feel like a real louse. "Could I really be so pathetic?" And the answer is yes. Admit that you love to wallow in hurt, bask in the limelight, or are trapped by guilt so that God can begin freeing you.

That's one of the beautiful things about the LASTS sequence. Just seeing, finally, that you tend to give control to the flesh in a certain area is the key step to taking the action that leads to God having authority in your life. Slowly, area by area, God's Spirit spreads His reign through your life as you yield to Him. That's sanctification, the slow conquest of your heart and will and the relentless overthrow of the power of the flesh in the willing Christian's life.

Submit

Making the choice here means that when you start to feel that little surge of hurt welling up inside, you stop and say, "No way!" You look instead to the truth about the situation you are in and consider the other person's needs as greater than your hurts. You'll discover that both of you find healing when you reject the flesh in this way and turn to the Spirit.

You might also have to turn down some ministry options to shut down the surge of positive fleshly power. As I told you previously, I have turned down some up-front ministry opportunities when I felt my motives were more fleshly than spiritual. I didn't come off looking very spiritual, especially since I didn't get into the whole internal rewards explanation to the people who might have noticed. But that's OK—God knew my motives, and the flesh was dealt a powerful blow.

You also need to make some choices where false guilt is concerned. You may have to take steps to disconnect from those people who are empowering your flesh by continually stimulating your negative internal rewards. They're manipulating you anyway, so why not distance yourself from them? Once again it may not seem spiritual or it may come across as hurtful to another person, but it is important to draw boundaries to limit negative effects from other people. If they are stimulating your flesh, put up a big "Keep Out!" sign.

Trust

It's part of the paradox of the Christian life that we must simultaneously do something and give up so much doing. There is a part you play in this—choosing to ask for God's rulership over an area you've previously given to the flesh—but for the rest you have to remember that you are not going to be able to do this on your own.

Your motives are deep and well hidden by your flesh. You can't even trust your feelings to tell you what motivates you because they have been corrupted through sin. What "feels right" is not always right anymore. If you are struggling and God has identified your inner motivations as a source of the problem, cry out to Him to change you deep inside by the power of His Spirit. You'll never change yourself. Trust Him to do it.

Dealing with guilt is going to take a specific kind of trust. You have to believe that when God says you are forgiven, you really are. You might not feel forgiven, but that's beside the point. You've also been feeling guilty, but that wasn't from God. Your feelings have been taken over by a liar, so you can't trust what they're telling you. Choose to trust in the One who forgave you.

Stand firm

This problem doesn't ever go away completely for any of us. Fleshly motives will always be there ready to take control. It's just as God explained it to Cain: "If you do what is right, will you not be accepted? But if you do not do what is right, sin is crouching at your door; it desires to have you, but you must master it" (Genesis 4:7, NIV). In other words, your flesh is forever crouching in the tall grass, waiting for the slightest opportunity to pounce. You must continually be skeptical of your motives.

To be able to hear the Spirit's voice as He motivates you to action, you must grow in spiritual maturity and discernment. How to you obtain this maturity? More often than not it is through times of difficulty. God will design circumstances that take away those positive feelings to show you where your motives originate. If your actions stay the same even when the earthly rewards went away, then you can see that your motives did not depend on the fleshly feelings. If your interest in carrying out a certain task disappears with the pleasurable responses, your motives were fleshly.

Take, for example, your desire to worship God during difficult times in your life. Do you lack a motivation to sing praises to God after you have lost your job? Do you hate the thought of going to church when you are struggling in your marriage? Now think about your feelings about the ministry you are involved in. When it does not seem as fun or rewarding, do you stay motivated? When the Sunday crowd is way down in attendance, are you depressed and seeking compensation elsewhere? Are you in it for your own internal pleasure sensations or to see people ministered to? Times of struggling will help purify your motives.

Don't run from God in times of struggling. Stay by His side, and stand firm. Internal rewards are tremendously strong areas of the flesh. You cannot combat them alone. You need to stay close to God in prayer, asking for His strength. Do not trust your own feelings, but test them against His Word. As we examine what God has told us in His Word, we can learn what we should find pleasure in, and meditating on those things will reprogram what gives us pleasure responses.

In time, we can find real pleasure in the things of God as we learn to trigger our internal rewards system when we are pursuing righteousness. We've all experienced it, that inner glow that comes when we're doing something we know pleases God. It's what Eric Liddell said in *Chariots of Fire*: "When I run, I can feel His pleasure."

Can you imagine what it would be like to be so God-oriented that we're dedicated to receiving positive feelings of reward from doing more and more things God delights in? You can get to this goal much faster if you hang out with people who give you encouragement in it. Just as others could direct you toward wrong behaviors with false guilt or peer pressure, Christians around you can stimulate the positive internal rewards to encourage you toward godly living.

You may ask, "Isn't this just more manipulation?" or "Wouldn't we then become addicted to good things—something you've been warning us about all along?" No, there is a difference.

If your motives are purified by the process we've outlined, then the godly actions your motives now encourage you toward will be consistent with the direction you are receiving in your Spirit, and no tension and struggle will result. You'll want to do God's will.

Over time, you can reverse the programming that sin has done in your internal fleshly processes and transform your internal system of rewards.

•CHAPTER 11

CONSCIOUS THOUGHT—RATIONAL THINKING AND THE WILL

CLARK (YEAH, IT'S ME)

"I'll take it!"

Three words I wish I could take back. But once spoken, they were like a genie coming out of its bottle. Once again I had obeyed my flesh, and once again I was going to pay for my mistake.

After I had completed medical school, I began my residency training. During that time I was trying to raise a young family on a very small income. It became necessary for me to have a car to get me back and forth to work. You know, one of those inexpensive but dependable "starter" cars that run well but don't look so great.

I went to a local car dealership and found exactly the car I needed. The paint was faded, the upholstery was torn, and it smelled a little funny inside. But it was in good running condition. Best of all, it was only $1,500. I comparison-shopped, checked the used car pricing guides, and felt it was a good deal. So after praying about it and feeling that it was right, I went to purchase the car.

While at the dealership, however, the helpful salesperson introduced me to "a true bargain." It was sweet: just one year old, driven by a little old lady only to church on Sundays. It was also a very professional-looking sedan, which was appropriate since I was, after all, a young professional. Best of all, it looked great. To top it all off, it was only $5,500—a real steal!

So there I stood looking between the slick, new yuppie car I yearned for and the dilapidated beater I'd be embarrassed to be seen in. I began to rationalize. Surely the extra expense for the newer car would be more than made up for by the fact that such a new car would need almost no repairs. And if my wife needed to drive it somewhere, I wouldn't worry about the thing breaking down on her. It was, in the end, more responsible to buy the more expensive car. Thus convinced, I turned to the ever-attentive salesman at my elbow.

"Well," I said, "I'd love to get into that new one. The problem is, I've only got $1,500."

"Are you kidding? That's no problem at all. Let's walk inside, and I'll let our financial guy explain all about instant credit."

I blinked at him. "You mean I can get the new one? Really?"

"My friend," he said with exaggerated friendliness, "you could drive it off the lot today."

I turned back to the beautiful car and uttered those three fateful words: "I'll take it!"

Less than one week after the ninety-day warranty expired, that car broke down. After it was repaired, it broke down again. And again. And again. Over the next few months it was in the garage more than it was on the road. Finally the mechanic told me I would have to replace the entire engine to solve the problems. So I shelled out the six hundred dollars for the new engine.

One week later, the transmission went. To replace it with a new transmission would cost $3,200, but for a used transmission it would cost only $1,800. I couldn't afford the car to begin with, and now this! I had to go with the used option. Shortly after the thirty-day warranty ran out on the used transmission, it stopped working. The replacement broke, too.

My "true bargain" was a true lemon. I was sure it was cursed. I looked to see if there had been a manufacturer recall on that model, but none existed. I went back to the dealership and asked them to purchase it back, but of course they wanted no part of it. And my supposedly good friend, the salesman, was nowhere to be found. It even crossed my mind to have it stolen or driven off a cliff, just to end the problem. But I was stuck with it, like an albatross around my neck.

Conscious Thought—Rational Thinking and the Will

MELANIE

Melanie is itching to have an affair. Her husband, a church elder, is far too busy with his church work and architecture firm to pay much attention to her. But it's not all his fault. Melanie's been eyeing the grass on the far side of the fence for years.

There's this man at church. Tom. She sees him every Sunday morning, Sunday night, and Wednesday night. His wife is sick a lot and often stays home. He's quite handsome and trim for a man with a young family.

Melanie doesn't know what it is, but she knows Tom's been giving off signals that indicate he's interested in her, too. Sometimes Melanie picks up Tom's kids at school and takes them to his house. Sometimes he does the same for Melanie. The last time he came, he acted like he didn't want to leave. They must've stood there at the front door for twenty minutes, just talking and laughing.

A part of her wanted to ask him inside. A part of her wished the kids hadn't been there.

She's been giving this a lot of thought. Of course, an affair would be disastrous. It would ruin not only her and her husband but also Tom and his family and ministry. After intense bouts of prayer and journaling, Melanie finally manages to squash the idea and get her heart back to the straight and narrow. She decides to avoid Tom from now on, giving off nothing but "not interested" signals.

But then Sunday rolls around, and there he is.

Did he just wink at me? Oh, my. Maybe I'm not as over this as I thought.

CONSCIOUS THOUGHT

OK, we're getting close to the end of our discussions of the physical realities of the flesh. This chapter covers one of the most interesting and perhaps least understood aspects of the flesh—conscious thought and its role in shaping our will.

Conscious thought and the will—those are things you have probably never considered to be connected to the flesh at all. They seem more associated to that eternal part of us, the soul or spirit, than the part that will perish at death. And how do we talk about conscious thought, anyway? It's pretty tough to visualize and define, even to the point of being a little spooky, so it is often lumped in with the metaphysical or the spiritual. But I assure you, it too is rooted in the fleshly functions of our bodies. Conscious thought and the will are as much a part of the flesh as our reflexes and hypothalamus are.

The problem in understanding conscious thought is that the idea of consciousness is itself somewhat difficult to, well, wrap your mind around. We've talked about all of the thousands of external and internal signals that race around your brain causing various reactions in your body. That seems clear enough. What is tough is to actually envision how one of these neurologic impulses stops being just an electric signal traveling through a nerve pathway and somehow breaks out of the subconscious realm and becomes a conscious thought.

Don't jump to the conclusion that this has to be purely spiritual simply since we don't understand it. While much of this process remains a mystery, we do know that a certain part of the brain—the cerebral cortex—is vitally important to conscious thought. When someone suffers damage to his cortex, the result is a decrease in consciousness. If conscious thought is so spiritual that it is not related to our physical bodies, why do brain injuries affect it?

A limited injury like a concussion will result in lethargy or confusion. A greater injury will result in temporary unconsciousness. Further injury to the cortex produces complete unconsciousness, or coma. If permanent, this is described as a *persistent vegetative state* where only the most basic functions of the lower brain centers are functioning. All of the body's various organ systems continue to function using subconscious pathways, but without the interactive and expressive features that we expect from a conscious person.

Obviously, the cerebral cortex—a very physical part of your fleshly body—governs much or all of your conscious thinking. It is no wonder, then, that Christians struggling with their flesh have long engaged in a "battle for the mind" when dealing with sin. This is because the lofty, "metaphysical" mind is firmly rooted in the flesh.

Along with the mind comes that poorly understood and often underused process we call *thinking*. We don't know a lot about what makes us able to build and fly airplanes when the rest of the animal kingdom walks around on webbed feet, furry toes, or hooves. Mostly it has to do with intelligence, and intelligence is really a measure of how fast your mind works.

Remember our neurologic pathways? Receiving-analyzing-responding. In the analyzing step, your brain compares new information with stored information to figure out the best response. Your brain sorts through all the data, and then, after thinking things through, it can make a rational decision. Now, think of it in terms of a race. If your brain can buzz through more options in a shorter amount of time than the next guy's brain, your brain is going to reach an answer more quickly. In the fleshly realm, quick thinking adds up to intelligence.

If you're having trouble accepting that something as lofty and spiritual as thought is actually a physical activity tied to your fleshly body, then remember that new imaging tools like positron emission tomography (PET) scans, single photon emission computed tomography (SPECT) scans, and functional magnetic resonance imaging (fMRI) allow us to see what portions of the brain are active when thinking. That's not to say your spirit is not involved. It may be, but let there be no doubt in your mind that "the mind" is rooted in the physical.

The Will

I just mentioned the neurologic pathway. The brain's amazing ability to go through the receiving-analyzing-responding cycle to come up with good responses to situations is an important aspect of the flesh. But conscious thought goes way beyond that. Conscious thought gives us the ability to reason and make decisions that go way beyond just selecting the most rational response to a stimulus. With conscious thought we are able to evaluate all our options and decide which we will *choose*.

This is perhaps man's greatest natural ability: the ability to exercise a free will.

The will is like the president sitting with his cabinet. He receives information from the Secretaries of State, Defense, Education, Homeland Security, Agriculture, Commerce, and the rest, and he considers all their input when a critical decision is at hand. The Secretary of the Treasury may counsel one way, the head of the Environmental Protection Agency another, and the vice president a third way altogether. In the end, it will be a choice of which of all of the opinions he will prioritize.

The will uses our conscious thought processes to evaluate the input from all of the fleshly resources we have discussed up until now and decides which options we will prioritize. The drives, reflexes, senses, subconscious impulses, emotions, and internal rewards are all considered, along with a review of what is rational. After all has been heard, the will decides which impulse will ultimately govern the decision.

Sometimes we make decisions to benefit us emotionally rather than physically, or we may do it to get a fleshly rush of sensation. Using our wills we can even make decisions that are absolutely contrary to rational thought: bungee jumping, for instance. When we go bungee jumping, we are ignoring the rational drives that urge us to preserve our own safety, and we are pursuing a strong fleshly sensation instead. A soldier might decide to fall on a grenade or a mother might decide to run into a burning building—not because the person's systems have concluded this is the best course of action for self-preservation, but because the will has decreed it is the most preferable thing to do, all things considered.

Or consider those times when we choose to deny our own emotions and suffer emotional hurt rather than hurt someone else. In such a situation we're not behaving rationally, strictly speaking. Sometimes even the Christian walk can seem to violate rationality: doing good to those who curse us, for example. It is all up to us. We have a truly free will.

Acts of the will are rarely as simple as I have described. Erratic emotions from the limbic system, racing thoughts in the cerebral cortex, hair-trigger conditioned responses, and the surges of impulse from the internal rewards system are all swirling around inside you. It's like choosing sides for an elementary school kickball game. Impulses from all over your flesh are jumping up and down screaming, "Pick me! Pick me!" Your will, the great ruler and judge, has to decide which impulse to prioritize.

This ability to overrule the other areas of the flesh is what gives the will its great power. It holds "absolute power" within the flesh. It is the supreme commander of all the flesh.

The Border of the Will's Kingdom

However, for all that, in the Christian's battle against the flesh, the will's power is actually pretty pathetic. There is power in having the authority to choose, but that's where the will's power ends. When it comes to getting your flesh whipped into shape, it has no power source to draw on to help change you. All it has to draw from is flesh.

More, all the choices it's choosing between and prioritizing are flesh choices. Whatever response it chooses will still only be a fleshly word, action, or perhaps a hormonal response to generate an emotion. And that's not much for the Christian to work with.

Weight loss is one of the best examples of willpower's weakness. The patients I have treated for obesity all come with the same story. They have tried every fad diet, weight-reduction plan, and motivational program available, and initially lost weight, only to regain it again. Maybe you have experienced this yourself. Willpower was strong enough to bring about a temporary change in their eating behavior. It was able to produce new conditioned responses or stronger rationalization to overcome whatever the problem was that made them overeat. But there was no lasting change. They put the weight back on—and then some—and added guilt, weariness, and frustration besides.

When they realize this, they come seeking medical help to find a stronger fleshly resource to overpower the underlying problem. And even then they often fail. Anyone who has tried to lose weight using only willpower knows how difficult it is to change even a simple fleshly behavior like eating.

The reason a non-Christian's will is so powerless here is that it can only choose between various fleshly functions. King Will cannot correct the damage from sin that corrupts the drives, reflexes, emotions, and other fleshly processes over which it presides. The best it can do is to choose the option that is the least corrupt or the least damaging.

That's what happened with Melanie in our story at the beginning of the chapter. Her fleshly drive for intimacy was pressuring her toward an affair. Her flesh served up several options for how to deal with her temptation, and her will had to choose which to go with. She was able to rationalize strongly enough to convince herself that an affair was a bad idea. She chose to avoid the guy. That was the best fleshly option her will had to choose from.

This resulted in good behavior in the short term, so it looked like willpower solved her problem, but no real change had happened inside her. The underlying problem was still there in her drives. Without the intervention of the Spirit in one or both of their lives, the outcome would likely be that the problem smolders and causes continued tension, or resurfaces when her fleshly rationalization is no longer able to contain her sin-corrupted drives. Maybe it will be with this guy; maybe someone else. The problem has just been swept under the rug. Only the Spirit can bring the reformation Melanie needs.

Impulsiveness

In chapter three we saw that the neurologic pathways that carry impulses to the cortex are very much like wires carrying information as an electrical signal. This makes them very, very fast. As soon as a sensor somewhere in your body is triggered, its signal rockets along the nerve pathways—and flesh is active. It will begin processing the information through its fleshly channels, running through all the options it sees and using all the information it has to reach a decision as quickly as it can.

This means you can often recognize the flesh's input just because it often arrives first. Ever prejudge someone or "jump to conclusions"? That may well be your flesh acting through your will to cause impulsiveness.

One day my wife came home with a new hairdo. She asked me what I thought of it. When I paused ever so slightly in my response, she jumped to a conclusion: "You hate it!" I actually liked it and was trying to come up with a really exciting way to say it to score some points, but my pause told her flesh that she didn't need any more input from me. It decided to generate a response based on the little feedback it had. The flesh is like that.

The responses that come "off the top of your head" are usually the flesh, too. Continuing on the hair theme, if you walk past someone on the street and suddenly feel the impulse to shout, "Hey, the '80s called, and they want their hairstyle back!" you should probably zip your lip. That's the flesh talking.

Rationalization

Back to the second step of the neurologic pathway again: analysis. That's where your brain analyzes incoming information and tries to come up with a good response. Well, when corrupted flesh is involved in this analysis, your will is going to look for good reasons to do bad things.

My car-buying story above is a good example. I knew what I *should've* done, but I really wanted that new car, the one that turned heads. And so my flesh set about to rationalize why I should buy the car that it wanted.

Smoking is another great example. I have had many patients who were ruining their health with cigarettes—some were even on the brink of death—yet they would not quit. Why? Because they had rationalized some reason for continuing to light up. "Oh, if I stop I'll gain weight." "Oh, I know it's caused my cancer, but the nicotine helps me cope with my illness." "Oh, I need them to help me relax." They had listened to the rationalizing arguments their fleshly minds had given them for continuing to do what their flesh wanted. As long as they were listening to their flesh, they would never be able to stop. The power fleshly rationalizing has to keep us in bondage is not to be underestimated.

Sound ridiculous to rationalize for the very thing that is harming you? Well, don't be too hard on the smokers. You and I do the same thing.

Treatment Plan

Listen

As you're listening for ways in which your will may be ruled by the flesh, examine your life for impulsiveness and rationalization.

One is the violation of the will ("I couldn't help myself"), and the other is the will violating good sense ("In the end I finally talked myself into doing it").

When you feel yourself wanting to act impulsively or make a spur-of-the-moment decision about something, beware! It's probably the voice of the flesh talking. The only good news about it is that when you *detect* that you're doing this and realize it's the flesh, you're on the path toward getting it turned over to God.

Another way to recognize that your flesh is in control of your actions is when you find yourself rationalizing. When you hear yourself explaining away the objections that stand in the way of you doing what your flesh wants, get a clue: your flesh may be ruling you in this area.

When the flesh and Spirit disagree within us about a decision, the flesh will be the one giving a list of explanations. The Spirit's answer is much more soft and certain. The result is that we can find ourselves rationalizing to try to have one of our other options approved and make our decision. The option that has more quick and loud "reasons" in its favor will usually be the one the flesh wants to go with.

I am not referring to the healthy practice of listing the pros and cons. This is also using the mind's power of rational thought, but in a controlled way. Nor am I saying that the Spirit's answer will always be the more distasteful option. I am referring to the times when you feel deep inside that one way is right, but you don't want to do it. So instead you try to convince yourself why the more likeable option is right by listing all the reasons for it, shouting down any reasons against it. Just like that silly guy in the car story above.

Whenever you stand at a crossroads and feel this unusual pressure urging you to rationalize for or against one of the paths open to you, it is generally a sign that the flesh is trying to influence the decision-making process. This is such a strong characteristic of the flesh that you can actually generate a good rule of thumb to help you figure out what the flesh is trying to get you to do: whatever you feel your mind trying to talk yourself into doing is probably the flesh's option.

The will given over to the flesh is a very dangerous thing. It has caused more bad choices—marriage-ending, family-destroying, career-ruining choices—than all other aspects of the flesh combined. When the chairman of the joint chiefs is corrupt, the whole system over which he presides is corrupt, too. Find where it's ruling you, and give it over to God.

When you work your way down to the God issue, you might find that you trust your own reasonings more than you trust God. You might just be too smart for your own good. Examine your relationship with the Lord, and see if you have any hang-ups with God hindering you.

```
Admit
```

So now, when we come to the confession stage, I'm not asking you to repent of using your mind in daily life. But if you find your decision making dominated by impulsiveness and rationalization, your flesh is in control of your will. And at whatever point the flesh controls you, it is sin.

As you would expect, this problem usually shows up in times of decision. You've thought through all the options and your mind has told you what it thinks you should do, but deep inside you have this nagging impression that it is wrong, so you are left struggling over the decision. Your flesh has one idea, and the Spirit is trying to tell you another. The more you look to the flesh for your decision, the more God will press His finger on your life and the more uncomfortable you will feel in the decision. If you can't recognize that pressure as His voice, you will be left struggling. If you turn and curse God for the discomfort you feel, you will be left really, *really* struggling.

So where is the sin in all of this? The problem is that you are comfortable with your own ability to reason, but you're not quite sure of that little Spirit nudge inside. The flesh lays out a whole list of reasons why it wants you to do the wrong thing, but the Spirit simply says, "Follow Me." If you have neglected your relationship with the Lord and lived a flesh-dominated life, you will know and trust—even love—the flesh's voice, but you will hardly recognize the voice of the Spirit. You have turned away from the loving God who wants to lead you like a gentle shepherd, and you have turned instead to the flesh. It is time to admit that as sin.

Submit

Now we come to an interesting discussion. All along through this book I've been talking about that tiny portion of this sanctification process that does rest in your power: the choice to submit this area to God's control. But how can you do that if your will—the very king of choosing—is enslaved to the flesh?

As King Will is holding court, all his fleshly subjects—homeostasis mechanisms, drives, reflexes, and the rest—parade before him for his review and selection. But for the Christian there is another source of input that King Will can choose from: the Spirit. Once God resides inside you, His voice is alive in your spirit and can be faintly heard among the rest of the flesh voices all shouting for recognition.

You see, the Christian's will remains sovereign. When God comes into your life, He doesn't *force* you to behave in certain ways. If you would rather choose to disobey God and follow the flesh, that's something He will let you do. Free will, remember? In the court of decision inside your mind, the option God would have you choose is laid before you beside all the other options. King Will sways his scepter over the whole array and finally chooses one option above all others. The Christian can choose God's way—while the non-Christian simply cannot (that option isn't one open to him)—but that doesn't mean the Christian always will choose God's way.

This is why it takes an act of the will to initiate God's work of salvation in your life. Don't get me wrong: no one comes to Jesus unless the Father draws him. But I mean the actual transaction of salvation: it will not commence until we make a decisive act of surrender to allow it. We don't call it "making a decision for Christ" for nothing. King Will has to submit to a greater authority. Salvation—surrendering to God and inviting Him to become Lord and Savior—is accomplished by grace through faith, and it is not of ourselves but is the gift of God. (See Ephesians 2:8.) Still, it is the will that is involved in the process.

The same is true of the whole Christian life. Sanctification, the regeneration of the flesh, requires many decisive acts of submission of the will in order to allow God to have lordship in your daily walk. Nor is the battle over with a single victory (or defeat). All along the way King Will can still decide to submit to the Lord's authority or resist. If you resist, your flesh regains control and will hinder His work of sanctification. If you choose to participate and submit your will to God, you allow His regenerating power to flow into your life to change you.

This is why we have seen that a choice of the will is needed in dealing with every characteristic of the flesh mentioned in previous chapters. At some point you need to *choose* not to be defensive, or emotional, or the rest. It is not the choice that brings change, but the choice conquers the power of the flesh and invites God to come in and make the change.

Trust

Getting your rational thinking under the Spirit's control is going to mean choosing to follow His leading even when it contradicts what you think. That is going to take trust. The smarter you are, the tougher this can be. As I said, intelligence is a matter of speed. Quick thinking can help on a math test, but it hurts when the Spirit is trying to get a word in edgewise. The smarter your flesh is, the faster it will interject its opinion. It's no wonder God often chooses the foolish things to confound the wise. The smart guys just don't listen.

But no matter how smart you are, your flesh always has an answer ready—and it never waits around to get the Holy Spirit's input. You're not going to grow in spiritual discernment as long as you're making decisions off-the-cuff. Sanctified decision making requires the use of your mind, but it must also include a prayerful pause in which you listen for the Spirit's input before making a final decision.

This is tough because of the flesh's quick thinking. Once we make a decision, even a hasty one, it's much harder to hear the Spirit's leading. It's as if we've closed our spiritual ears to any more discussion. When the flesh is active, we tend to cling to our conclusions just to avoid that uncomfortable state of confusion and paralysis that exists before a decision is made. Sometimes it's easier to go with what might be a wrong decision rather than remain indecisive. So we boldly press on in the flesh without the input of the Spirit just to avoid further deliberating. But when we do so, we give the flesh full control of our decision making. Simply waiting a while before making a final decision will help. Sleep on it.

The Spirit's answer, on the other hand, is almost always slower in coming. Not because God is slow, but because our spirits are slow in receiving His message. Some answers arrive only after much prayer and consideration. This takes time. The flesh, not exactly brimming with patience, hates this delay.

Many times I have cried out to God for something, wanting information or a change right then, only to have the answer be, "Wait." *Ick*. Usually, however, the time spent waiting is when God is preparing me to receive and accept His answer. All the while, however, the impulsive flesh is screaming, *I want an answer now!* Or rather, *I want you to choose my option now!*

Trusting God requires putting a lid on the fleshly responses and waiting for His answer. In fact, He's probably already given you the answer. Sort through all the options, discard the ones generated by the fleshly processes you now understand, and look for that one that can't be explained in fleshly terms. It is probably God's voice. Once you've identified it, step out and follow in trust.

Stand firm

As you are waiting for that final victory in dealing with your fleshly decision making—or any other area of the flesh—you need to rely on God to do an inner work to bring about change. You will not defeat the flesh with willpower. There simply is not much power at King Will's command. Now you know why. The will has the power to choose, but that's about it.

Not that that's a bad thing. You can use the will to make good choices and solve some problems. I think this is what secular counseling does. If a counselor can help you see that you are choosing a destructive lifestyle and encourage you to use your will to make a new choice, that's great. Don't be confused when non-Christian friends say, "I don't need God; I found the same help in my therapist as you find at church." That's just flesh helping flesh, and in some things that can work.

You don't have to go very far in life, however, to find that the flesh's power to change itself is very limited. The urges rising up from within Melanie, above, need to be changed, not just her outward feelings. And you need change deep inside too, in places you could never change with your own ability to reason. We really do need strength from outside ourselves, from the Spirit, to bring change in life's most distressing problems.

We all have tried to change distressing behaviors on our own—those repeating, habitual bad habits that keep getting us in trouble but won't ever seem to go away. Maybe that's one reason you picked up this book. Whatever your ingrained sin problem—outbursts of anger, sexual drivenness, defensiveness, jealousy, gambling, uncontrollable impulsiveness, overeating—it is impossible to gain lasting victory over it in your own strength. We can decide to stop, determine to change, and promise that "this will be the last time" as often as we like, but if we rely only on the power contained in our will, we will fail.

When times of struggling with the flesh are dragging on, it is not time to try one more round of willpower. You're fighting a war of attrition, and it is time to starve your flesh and nourish your spirit. Do whatever you can to stay out of the situation where you will be faced with your difficult decision. If it involves a person, stay away from her. If it is a substance, stay away from where it is sold or stashed. If it is a decision, forget it for a while.

Then it is time to stand firm by nourishing your spiritual life. This requires growing in your relationship with the Lord through prayer, study of His Word, worship, and fellowship. Finding lasting victory will require the Spirit doing an inner work to sanctify the corrupt flesh that is driving you. Then your will can have sanctified fleshly responses to choose from in daily life interactions, and good responses will naturally flow.

THE CURE

SECTION 3

CHAPTER 12

THE FINAL HEALING

Adam and Evelyn

Adam walks through the door and drops his keys in the bowl on the table. "Evelyn, honey, I'm home."

She comes in from the kitchen and gives him a kiss. "Mmm. Welcome home. How was your day?"

"It was good. We'll talk about it in a minute," he says. "But first, I want to ask you something."

She smiles curiously. "Ask me."

"Well, it's our anniversary next week, you know. And I was thinking we'd go to a certain restaurant to celebrate. I've already arranged a sitter." He studies her face hopefully. "What do you say?"

The corners of Evelyn's lips turn down. She lets out a heavy sigh. "Sure."

His forehead furrows. "What? Don't you want to go?"

"Sure. Fine, fine. It'll be great." She looks at him, her eyes narrowed. "Anything would be better than the year you forgot our anniversary completely."

Adam pulls back as if struck. "What?"

"Do you know I still get a deep ache inside every time I think about it?" she asks, a tear forming in her eye.

He drops his arms from her waist. "Not that again. Are you going to ruin yet another anniversary with that old problem? Why do you always have to throw it in my face? I messed up, all right? I said I was sorry like a hundred times. I've never forgotten again.

What more do you want from me?"

"Me ruin it? What about you?"

And so it continues, going from bad to worse.

Analyze This

Did you see the flesh at work? Could you see it in her reaction, in her choice to dwell on the deliciously terrible feeling the memory generates? Could you spot it in his decision to escalate? Allow me to dissect it.

When Adam suggests they go to dinner for their anniversary, Evelyn receives the auditory stimulus, and it goes right from the receptors in her ears to her brain. It is passed through the subconscious brain centers, and a match is made with a memory from many years ago when Adam forgot their anniversary. The signal is sent to the limbic system, where it is analyzed and associated with the emotion of sadness. This signal is then sent to the temporal lobe of the cerebrum, and sad responses are generated and sent out. The corners of the lips turn down, and the lungs take in a deep breath and release a sigh.

As the fateful comment continues to be analyzed in Evelyn's mind, the subconscious center notes a chemical marker attached to this memory, indicating that it is important. The marker was attached by a chemical reaction with adrenaline, which was present when the memory was originally stored because it was during an argument over the subject. Recognizing the importance of the signal, the lower brain center sends the signal up to the cerebral cortex to reach conscious thought. Suddenly, Evelyn consciously remembers the previous incident when their anniversary was forgotten. After barely perceptible conscious analysis, signals are sent back to the limbic system confirming and reinforcing the previous signals of the emotion of sadness. All this has occurred in the milliseconds that followed her husband's comments, even while the words still hung in the air.

The final loop of the neural pathway sends the signal back up to the cortex to generate the question, "How will I respond next?" Everything so far has been involuntary and lightning fast. The spontaneous steps of the neural pathway are completed. The next step, however, will require a choice, so the will is called into action.

The will now examines the available information. The only sensory information is the auditory input from Adam's words about their upcoming anniversary. Few words were received, but this stimulus is carefully analyzed for every tone and inflection to determine the precise meaning of his statement and to interpret any associated meaning or attitude attached to the statement. The memories of the forgotten anniversary and the emotion of sadness are considered, right along with a still, small voice coming from the Spirit: "Forgive as you have been forgiven." The will must decide which impulse will take priority when deciding on a response.

A fraction of a second passes.

Without additional thought, Evelyn decides to give priority to the negative emotional input she's feeling and responds, "Anything would be better than the year you forgot our anniversary completely." Why did she give almost no consideration to other options? Because for the last ten years since the anniversary was forgotten, she has always given the same response. Now it is almost a reflex to give her conditioned response. The amount of time needed to determine this response to the anniversary issue has been reduced to almost nothing.

With her own words just leaving her mouth, she now calls to memory her feelings of hurt, and she uses them to produce the re-stimulation of the emotional neural pathways and recycle the feelings of sadness. This time it is initiated by Evelyn's own choice. After initiation, however, the process is no longer under her control, but under the control of the flesh. She made the choice to hand the keys to the flesh, and now it's driving the bus. The neural pathways will function according to their predetermined programming to produce new responses.

The stimulus travels back to the limbic system, where the emotion of hurt is produced to add to the sadness. Additional signals are sent out to produce physical responses to show hurt. The body posture slumps and the head drops. A tear forms in the eyes. All of the body's systems then report back that the appropriate responses have been generated, and they look for more directions.

As the neurologic pathway spins one more time, a signal again returns to the conscious mind to determine the next response. It is time for another choice.

Evelyn reanalyzes the situation. The rational, sensory, and emotional stimuli are rushing through her brain. The still, small voice can barely be heard amidst all the stimulation from the flesh. Her rational mind tells her she is quite justified in feeling hurt. This generates a deeply satisfying sensation in the system of internal rewards, so this response pathway is given priority by the will. A decision is made to prioritize the feelings of hurt, so an early stress response is initiated as her body prepares to lash out in counterattack. A slightly bigger surge of stimuli is experienced by the flesh, strengthening its effects and reinforcing its control.

"I get a deep ache inside every time I think of it," she replies, now with a sharp edge on her voice put there by a small surge of adrenaline. It is true that she gets a deep ache. What she does not tell him, because she does not recognize it herself, is that she—not Adam—initiated that deep ache this time. Choosing to dwell on the memories of hurt sent them back through her limbic system to intensify the internal reward sensations.

Even as she speaks these words there is a small voice deep inside her calling for an honest assessment of her feelings. It points out that she actually *likes* this deep ache somehow, and even promotes it. She cannot quite put her finger on where that thought came from—it is the language of the Spirit, not the flesh—so she ignores it. Instead, there is a fresh round of fleshly impulses that surge through her as a result of her last statement, until the signals again return to her conscious mind.

By the time the signal again returns to the woman's cortex to again ask the question, "What next?" Adam has had time for his flesh to respond.

"Not that again!" he replies, setting up his defensive posture to counter her attack. "Are you going to ruin another anniversary with that old problem?"

Now Evelyn has a new external stimulus to respond to. This time it's a perceived threat. "Is he really suggesting that this is my fault?" she asks herself as she uses fleshly reason to analyze the input from her husband. "If he is going to imply that it is my fault, then he has another think coming!" is the response generated after her analysis, and she sends a new signal to her own neural pathways. This time it is anger.

The limbic system lights up. A rush of chemicals washes through the lower brain centers. A strong sense of anger is added to hurt and sadness. These feelings are rationalized as being entirely justified, and there is a deep sense of satisfaction in feeling them.

Now there is an outright accusation against her. This threat must be countered. The nervous system is now on full-scale alert. A signal goes out to the hypothalamus, then the pituitary, then all the glands of the body. Every organ system is readied for the fight. Adrenaline floods through the body, calling on every system to heighten its activity. The lungs are heaving, the heart pounding, the mind racing.

The still, small voice in the woman cries out, "A gentle word turns away wrath," but it no longer can be heard. The flesh is in full control.

The events from here on are programmed and predictable. Attack, defend, and counterattack. Continue to battle until the fight is won. It is a matter of protecting your territory, striving to get what you need, and fending off attackers. It is so fleshly and animalistic you might as well be out in the woods. The only possible result is injury and pain.

So goes life when we're ruled by the flesh.

A Final Dose

As my last act as your doctor, I would like to speak a helpful, but brutal, truth into your life. It may hurt to hear it, and it may fly counter to some things you've heard in church. But I assure you, this is the kind of pain that leads to great healing. If you can truly embrace this insight, it will be revolutionary for you. And remember, it applies to me, too.

All right, here goes.

In these pages I hope I have removed the illusion that you are some great spiritual being who just happens to be momentarily trapped in a physical shell and periodically tormented by a "little old man of the flesh" inside. Nothing could be further from the truth. From the time we were created as Adam and Eve, we have been flesh. From head to toe you and I are saturated with the stuff of this temporal realm. You live, breathe, and eat the muck of this fallen world. You are a hodgepodge of wires and chemicals, receptors signaling, and muscles and glands responding. You are driven to and fro by physical processes you don't even understand. Your human nature is not something residing in you—it is you. You are human.

Well, how'd you hold up? It wasn't that bad, was it? Still, it hurts to think of yourself that way, doesn't it? You might be concerned that such a low view of yourself as a human creature is somehow going to disrupt the victorious Christian image you have been taught to imagine. Not by a long shot. When you finally come to this realization, it is going to change you. And it will be a far better change than you might expect. This honest view of yourself is not going to keep you from being victorious—it is going to make victory possible.

How? It is going to allow you to throw off false pretense and get you to the place where God can begin a genuine work of sanctification in your life. It is going to get you to the place Paul tells us sanctification begins: with the declaration, "Wretched man that I am! Who will separate me from this body of flesh?" (See Romans 7:24.) So long as you think you're doing just fine and are in no need of help, you will never grow beyond these stubborn sins.

So if this new understanding of the flesh has left you feeling wretched, don't despair: you are at a good place. You may be buckling under the weight of the flesh in your life, but there is hope for you. You have been sent a Savior. And now that you are ready to put no confidence in your worthless fleshly attempts to rid yourself of sin, you are ready to accept your Savior's help. You are ready to identify the sin that still controls you, fully repent of it, and rely on the indwelling power of the Holy Spirit to thoroughly cleanse you of it. As you do, you will find that the problems that once held you in a death grip will weaken and fall from your life as you are set free from their power.

The result will be no more confusion, condemnation, or consternation over the flesh in your life.

No More Confusion

This revelation of the flesh was a dramatic one for me that blew away so many of the illusions that had clouded my understanding of the way the flesh and Spirit work in our lives. It was like Neo being unplugged from the Matrix for the first time and seeing the reality of the world around him. It was a hard revelation, but when it fully sunk in, suddenly things made a lot more sense.

In fact, the fleshly world we live in is very similar to the Matrix described in the movie. In the movie, all the humans had a wire plugged into their brains that connected them to a master computer. The computer fed them information about a virtual reality world they thought they lived in, when really they were slaves to the enemy machines.

The same is true for us. There are no enemy machines, but all of what we perceive to be reality is fed into our minds by wires from all of our sensory receptors. It creates a whole world of images, smells, and tastes as we live in this world of flesh. But just like the movie, this is not the whole reality. Morpheus described the Matrix as "the illusion pulled over your eyes to blind you from the truth." So is the flesh an illusion pulled over your spiritual eyes to blind you from the spiritual reality all around you. As we learn to reject the distractions of the flesh, we can more fully experience all that God has for us spiritually.

Now that we have thoroughly described the flesh as a real and living thing that you can identify in your life, you can get unplugged from it just as in the movie. You won't be disconnected to move into another realm, at least not yet. That will come when you die and are ultimately disconnected from the flesh and you move freely into the spiritual realm into heaven. For now, becoming unplugged occurs as the reality of the flesh takes hold and you suddenly wake up and see it functioning in your life.

The flesh will no longer be able to hide in your life. You can kick out that "little old man of the flesh" illusion. You will now see the flesh clearly whenever it tries to control your thoughts and actions. You won't need to go through the struggling that Evelyn is going through in our story above. As those symptoms of repetitive conflict become apparent, you will see that the flesh is at work.

Feeling a little defensive as your ministry suggestion is being discussed by the church board? Your plans were going along quite smoothly until Brother Stonewall decides to throw a wrench in things and throw off your homeostasis. *Aha!* You will now recognize that this means your flesh is active and that it is time to get those feelings under control. Let Brother Stonewall criticize if he wants; with your flesh subdued and the Spirit in control, there is no need to launch a counterattack. God is in control of your ministry, and He will have His way, you can rest assured.

Fighting with the wife over the purchase of that boat you just have to have? That driven feeling deep inside is the signal that your flesh is the source of your marital conflict, not your wife's lack of submission. Do a little digging, and you might find the pressure stemming from a desire to keep up with Lenny from work who just bought a boat, and deeper still you might find resentment against God for not giving you all the luxuries your non-Christian (non-tithing) co-workers have. Well, that bit of flesh is not going to hide any longer. You've identified it and subdued it, and you wife will thank you for it.

In a similar way, you will recognize the reflex responses, sensory addictions, subconscious programming, emotional pressure, internal rewards, and rationalization whenever they surface in your life, and you will know the flesh is at work causing problems.

When God drives home the understanding of how the flesh works, you will receive sudden insight into the world around you. It will be a revelation, an epiphany, unlike anything you've experienced in a long time. The world will become clear to you. The news will become clear. Your own behavior will become clear. New eyes will see new things, and you'll be blown away. You'll wonder how this thing could have been going on all around you for so long and you'd never been able to see it.

You'll also be able to recognize the flesh at work in others. If you happen to be the wife in the abovementioned boat-purchasing discussion, an understanding of the flesh will make your husband's drivenness stand out like Marilyn Manson at the Southern Baptist convention.

Just wait until the next time you are at a church service and see someone performing up front with the beaming facial expressions and body posture of a person basking in the glow of his or her own internal rewards. It'll make you sick—not because the person is nauseating, but because you realize that your fleshly attempts at spirituality are just as stomach turning.

One word of caution as you begin to recognize the flesh in others: the flesh is a wild animal, and you are wise to not corner it when you see it in others. Your best response whenever you encounter uncontrolled flesh will be to stop and examine where the other person's flesh has stimulated your flesh and get yours under control. Throwing two unrestrained fleshly beasts into an argument is like starting a cockfight. You'll claw each other to death without accomplishing anything. Once your flesh is under control, you can gently encourage the other person to evaluate his and continue your interactions under the control of the Spirit.

You should also never be confused about why bad things happen to good people anymore. First, you can see that none of us is really good. We are all fleshly to the core and in need of sanctification. But more importantly, you can see that as Christians the *bad things* can really be *good things* that God is using to help you become more sanctified and grow in your relationship with Him. The promise to "use all things together for good" refers to what *He* considers good. His good things are not just the things that make you happy or feel good. That is the flesh's goal for maintaining everything in a nice happy state of normalcy with no interruptions—remember homeostasis?

There's another thing you should no longer be confused about—God's primary goal is not to make you happy. He is not out there trying to bend every natural law of the universe so that you feel good. And isn't that just what we want? The minute we are sick we run to God and say, "Supernaturally heal me!" Just look at any prayer chain list, and you will find 80 percent or better sound something like this: "Aunt Tilly broke her hip and needs healing." "Brother Bob lost his job and needs another." "The Jeffersons are going on vacation and want traveling mercies so their car doesn't break down."

Do you notice anything? It is all fleshly comfort that we ask for. Believe it or not, God is not primarily concerned with making you healthy or fulfilled in your job or even to have all your needs met by your spouse. He has much bigger goals in mind.

Do you remember the original design God had for placing us in this physical world? It was to give us a place to choose Him over the flesh. And the minute God sends some struggle into our lives to free us from the flesh, we say, "No! I love the flesh. Give me back my fleshly comforts!" He must shake His head in wonder at our choice.

"But I thought God wants to meet our every need, just like He takes care of the sparrows," you may wonder. That's true, but the problem is that when we are in bondage to the flesh, we want Him to give us only what we *want* physically, not what we *need* spiritually. God knew that the prodigal son needed to spend some time in the pigsty. The important thing is that the pigsty was a very good thing for the prodigal, because it was the only way he was going to be reunited with his father. Struggling can be just what you need in your life at times.

When you finally take hold of this understanding, your perspective on every circumstance in life will change. Your focus will no longer be about meeting your needs and eliminating discomforts in the flesh. Now you will look for the spiritual goals in every situation. You won't be sidetracked by the good fleshly feelings in times of victory or devastated by the bad fleshly impulses when there are problems.

Then when it comes time for prayer requests, your aching back and broken-down car won't be the first thing on your mind anymore. You will be asking God what new work He is trying to do in you in your particular circumstance, and you will be looking forward to a deeper relationship with Him as a result. When your prayers start reflecting your desire to have more pleasure in Him and less in the flesh, you will know you are getting somewhere.

No More Condemnation

Something else dramatic happens as you begin to see the flesh for what it really is: you also see sin for what it really is.

As we have said, sin is what happens whenever the flesh controls your actions. This definition works well for what is typically thought of as sin. Your fleshly drives make you take what you need by going out and stealing, and we call that a sin. It also helps us to understand things that we might not typically think of as sin, but still lead us into stubborn problems. Your involvement in church ministry, for example. It's no wonder it has caused you so much struggling if you are doing it only to generate some pleasant internal reward. It is flesh—and it is sin.

This understanding is going to help you sweep away some illusions about things that are not sin that you might have been feeling false guilt over. Feeling bad for turning down a church responsibility because you want to devote more time to your family? Now you can see that your motives are pure and that saying *yes* would actually be just to please some unpleasable person at church.

Keep in mind that the flesh itself is not bad. It was created by God to allow you to live in this physical world, but it has become corrupted by sin and needs sanctification. And sanctification means getting it under the control of the Spirit. When the flesh is helping you live out your life here on earth under the control of the Spirit, it is just as God created it—it is good.

Eating is an example of a good and necessary fleshly event. When it is out of control, it becomes gluttony and is a sin. Sex within the confines of God's plan for marriage is a good thing. But pursue it outside of marriage, and it becomes fornication or adultery, which are sins. Sin occurred because flesh took control and corrupted something that was otherwise good. The important point is that we should not say that all fleshly pleasures are sin. When they are enjoyed under the control of the Spirit, they are wonderful blessings given to us by God, and there is no need for condemnation in enjoying them.

The Christian life, then, is no longer a struggle to follow a set of imposed rules; it is a struggle with the flesh. In fact, Paul tells us that living the Christian life is not at all about living under law anymore: "'I am allowed to do all things,' but I will not let anything make me its slave" (1 Corinthians 6:12, NCV). Now it is about what controls you. Get your focus off of trying to live within a set of rules to avoid sin. No matter how much willpower you muster up, you can't do it anyway. And start identifying where the flesh needs to be gotten under control. The result is no more condemnation.

We won't throw out rules completely. There is one benefit to them. Rules may not sanctify the flesh, but they can contain it. Before someone is able to truly sanctify his flesh, it can be temporarily restrained by rules. We do this with children. We give them a set of rules to live by until they grow up and learn to control their actions themselves. We can do the same with young Christians by giving them guidelines for how to live and function as a Christian until the work of sanctification produces maturity and these good works spontaneously.

Notice that restraining the flesh with legalism is for the immature. We must not stay there. If we stay in this immature state, the result is inevitable failure because the caged animal of the flesh will not remain in its cage of law for long. It will eventually break out, and its programmed fleshly nature will take over. This is why so many are locked in fear and condemnation when struggling with sin. They are afraid God will reject them for breaking some law. They have never moved on to a mature perspective that understands that sin will never be conquered unless the fleshly nature is changed by a work of God in their lives.

Once you have been freed from the law and pursue the Spirit controlled-life, you find that even when you fail and the flesh controls you, there is still no room for condemnation. Paul concludes his classic discussion on the flesh in Romans 7 with the triumphant declaration, "There is therefore now no condemnation to them that are in Christ Jesus" (Romans 8:1, ASV). If you are in Christ, you are covered. Yes, you are still human, so don't be surprised when your flesh rises up and takes control and makes you struggle. That just means you're alive.

So don't waste time or energy on guilt when you are struggling. Stand firm in your battle against the flesh, and know that God is still at work and that He will accomplish real changes deep in your flesh that result in new, sanctified behaviors. It may take some rebalancing of hormones or rewiring of your neurologic pathways, but this is no problem for God. The same power that accomplished salvation in your life is available to flow through your flesh and bring regeneration there as well.

Also, don't waste time looking for the complete eradication of the flesh. Since the flesh is so thoroughly linked to your physical being, you will have it with you as long as you live. I like the way Martin Luther put it: "When we shall finally stop [sinning], we shall have become pious, that is, when they use the shovel to put us under ground."[1] The goal is not the elimination of the flesh. That won't occur until the final step of our spiritual journey, glorification, when we enter heaven.

The goal and end result of sanctification will be living here in this physical world still with fleshly functions managing the events of our lives, but under the control of the Spirit.

No More Consternation

You will never eliminate the flesh and find sinless perfection in this life, but you can find relief from the feelings of wretchedness, turmoil, and helplessness that occur as symptoms of struggling with your flesh. The battle with the flesh continues, but it no longer produces the struggles it used to because it no longer consumes your whole attention.

The goal of your battle with the flesh originally was just to eliminate problems from your life. Now it becomes a quest to go deeper into a spiritual relationship with God. You have seen what the flesh will do when it controls your life, and you despise it. Now you will no longer be satisfied with anything but a Spirit-controlled life.

Armed with your new understanding of the flesh, you will find yourself identifying and defeating many of the fleshly responses that have produced so many problems for you in the past. Where they still exist, they will not cause the harm they once did because you have become astute to their presence and you know when they are functioning. You can easily recognize the defensiveness, drivenness, and conditioned responses that characterize the flesh, and you know how to turn instead to the Spirit for healing that LASTS.

As you have been listening, admitting, submitting, trusting, and standing firm, the power of the flesh has been waning. The more you persist, the weaker it becomes, and piece by piece the flesh in your life will be brought under the control of the Spirit. Eventually, the fleshly comforts in life become unimportant, and your primary concern is what happens between you and God. Accomplishing God's spiritual objectives for your life will become your top priority.

To see what this looks like in reality, let's look at David. Here is a guy who struggled. He had years of tension while he hid from Saul, who threatened to kill him, and then more turmoil over his sin with Bathsheba. Plus oppression, even outright depression, over the death of his son that followed. He was a steadfast child of God, and God allowed struggling to bring David closer to Him.

Later in life, after years of struggling had produced the inner workings of sanctification, David ended up facing yet another struggle. This time his own son, Absalom, was the one from whom he was fleeing. As David fled Jerusalem for the wilderness, a relative of Saul named Shimei chased after him hurling insults: "Get out, get out, you man of bloodshed, and worthless fellow!" (2 Samuel 16:7). Shimei apparently was one of the first-known mudslinging politicians because all the time he was cursing David, he was also hurling stones and dirt to further demean him.

What did David do in response? Nothing, and the cursing and mudslinging continued. Finally, Abishai, one of David's mighty men, had had enough. He turned to David and said, "Why should this dead dog curse my lord the king? Let me go over now and cut off his head" (2 Samuel 16:9).

Before we look at what David said in response, let me ask you a question. Now that you understand the characteristics of the flesh, what would a fleshly response be?

The flesh would have wanted to remove this source of discomfort as quickly as possible, just as Abishai suggested. It would have been very easy to use fleshly rationalization to justify "defeating those who offend the Lord's anointed" and "shutting the mouths of those who curse," and all the while sounding pretty spiritual. He could have pointed out Shimei's error and invoked all sorts of Scripture about authority and obedience and justified having Shimei quieted. He could have easily comforted himself in having Shimei killed by saying that Abishai's act of loyalty was a good thing that resulted from the situation. But he did not.

His response was, "Let him alone and let him curse, for the Lord has told him. Perhaps the Lord will look on my affliction and return good to me instead of his cursing this day" (2 Samuel 16:11-12). David looked past the problem blaring in his face and saw that God was at work in it. He did not rush to eliminate the problem. Instead, he waited to see what good thing God would do through it.

The result for David was that the cursing continued. There was no quick or easy way out of the discomfort, even after he gave a good, Spirit-led response. In fact, Shimei's cursing followed him all the way along his journey to his destination, but it did not cause David to struggle inside. The sensory stimulation evoked no fleshly response. He looked past the current problem and looked only to what purposes God had for him. He was now living outside the fleshly Matrix.

You may hope that at the end of struggling you find a place of euphoric happiness, of complete sinlessness, but this is not the case. Remember that the extremes of emotion are a fleshly response, not spiritual. A Spirit-controlled life is one of greater constancy. There are times of joy and of sorrow, but they are the deep and abiding inner sensations of the Spirit. The high times are seen for the fleshly emptiness that they possess. The low times of struggle are endured and overcome until they no longer generate the terrible fear and despondency. Watchman Nee describes it this way:

> Christians nowadays incline too strongly towards a life of feeling. If God should take away the joyous feeling, they would lose everything. Yet God does not say to live by feeling, but He says to live by faith. After years of experience you will come to realize that joy and dryness are really the same. No great outburst of joy will affect you, nor will any moment of dryness influence you. You live the same life though deep aridity as well as through great joy.
>
> Oh that we may not act like those with a small capacity—in joy they dance in the house; in dryness they drench the wall with tears. If we live by faith we shall not be swayed by either of them. Even so, let it be plainly understood that we are not people without emotion. We do have feelings of

joy as well as of dryness. But we ought not allow these external sensations to touch our inward man.[2]

The result of sanctification will be that your emotions and every other fleshly impulse will come finally under the control of the Spirit. You will reach a place where neither the highs nor the lows will distract you from your commitment to your relationship with God. Winning is fine. Losing is fine. It is all ordained by God. You will be able to say with Paul, "To live is Christ and to die is gain" (Philippians 1:21). Ease or hardship, pleasure or pain, even living or dying—they are all the same when the rantings of the flesh have been replaced by the quiet assurance of the Spirit-led life.

It is at this point that you have accomplished victory over the flesh and have found the end of struggling.

CONCLUSION

WHEN you come to understand how the flesh works, you'll begin to see it everywhere. Of course you'll see it in yourself. Praise God! You'll spot it very quickly and be able to bring it under the withering wind of God right away. But you'll also see it all around you. It will be as if you have been given new eyes, and suddenly you truly see.

You'll see it in your co-workers—the one who loves to receive the rush from acceptance and affirmation from the boss, and the other who loves to be seen as the first, best, and smartest.

You'll see it in the news. When a husband is accused of killing his wife and the investigation discovers that there was an affair going on that the wife had confronted him about, you'll remember that when the flesh's supply of good feelings is threatened, a person is capable of violating any boundary.

You'll see it in world events. Presidential elections are notorious for bringing the flesh front and center. Decades of violence in countries steeped in revenge. Notorious forgeries, lies, and betrayals. Maybe it's actually the flesh that makes the world go 'round.

You'll see it in the Bible, too. Look at King Saul. He was king. Everyone adored him. He was all but worshiped. But then along came this upstart, David, and suddenly Saul's drug of choice was in short supply. People's heads swiveled away from him and toward David. People praised this ruddy youth. Women made up songs praising David's deeds. And suddenly Saul was a raving maniac, capable of killing not only David but also his own son.

Look at the Pharisees in the New Testament. They loved the chief seats at the synagogue, the respectful greetings in the marketplace, and being called *rabbi*. They had it rich. Then along came this country preacher, Jesus, taking away their crowds! Now people didn't look at them with respect anymore. Now the pews were empty, and everyone had gone out to *Him*. And they found themselves lying, conniving, conspiring, and arranging any kind of trap possible to get rid of this man.

Not only will you be able to see the flesh in action around you, but you willl also notice when people have the flesh in check.

Consider John the Baptist. His ministry drew large crowds. Everyone streamed out to the desert to hear John speak. You can imagine them hanging on his every word. If anyone ever had all the conditions necessary for becoming addicted to his flesh, it was John. Then along came Jesus, and John dutifully pointed people to Him—and they went. After a while, John's disciples came to him and said, "Hey, you've lost your audience! Everybody's gone over to that other guy. Why not do some stunt to get them back?"

John's response is a challenge to all of us who desire to have God in perfect charge of our flesh: "He must increase, but I must decrease."

Isn't that what you long for? I know that's what I want in my life. That stubborn sin (or *sins*, if you're like me) has been keeping you down. Your flesh has been driving the bus—and causing accidents beyond number. But with the flesh in check, you can walk through this world and not be ensnared by its many charms. You can step into those situations that used to cause you to stumble and instead react in the spirit. You can throw off the sins that so easily entangle and run to Jesus where He waits at the finish line.

You can have purity that LASTS.

Your Mission Begins

There's an old Baptist encampment in New Mexico, called Glorieta. As you drive out the gates and head toward the highway, you pass one last sign from the camp: "Your mission begins." You may have come to Glorieta for healing, teaching, and meditation, but once you leave, the real work begins. So it is with us.

Conclusion

We have come at last to the end of our journey together. You came to me complaining of certain discomforts. We soon identified those discomforts as areas in which the flesh was ruling you. The patterns of stubborn sin, we found, were actually God's way of showing you where problems lay. That turmoil you felt about it was God's finger pressing on the spot He wanted brought under His control. Together we explored the physiological systems at work in the recurring problem and found a solution that LASTS.

Now we're about to part company. I hope you realize that you were not only the patient in this medical discussion, but also the medical student. From here on you will be on your own to go forth into a world rife with temptations that seek to entice your flesh. But you're not the same now, are you? Now you've learned how the flesh works. I imagine you can see it at work all around you: in you, your spouse, your friends, your children—even celebrities and world leaders. And now you are equipped to help some of them, starting with you.

None of us will reach moral perfection this side of heaven. But with the understanding you now have, and equipped with the LASTS pathway for bringing the flesh under God's control, you know how to walk in ever-increasing personal holiness. The time between sin and freedom will get shorter and shorter. You will quickly see new areas of fleshly control and bring them to the cross of Christ. The sin that so easily entangles will have less and less hold on you. And your most stubborn of sin strongholds will ultimately be toppled by God's Spirit.

I hope you have received something even greater than conquering sin in your life in what you have read. Remember back to the Garden of Eden, when God placed us in this physical realm to reject the enticements of the flesh and choose Him.

My prayer is that through what you have read here you will see that defeating the flesh is not about making you more acceptable to God. You can't be any more acceptable to Him than you already are! Rather, this has been about a way to be more in love with Him.

Making you free from sin is not an issue anymore. Christ did that on the cross. We've been talking about the work of *sanctification* that the Great Physician will do in your life—but which you can join with Him in. Take what you have learned here to get loose from those entanglements of the flesh, so you can more fully love your Savior.

Stubborn sins are what hold us back from the kind of walk with Christ we desire. The flesh keeps us in bondage and sabotages our most godly aspirations. It's the kind of misery Paul complained about in Romans 7. And it's no way to live. My prayer is that you will find in this book the help you need to finally kick off those chains and run free at the side of your Master.

NOTES

CHAPTER 2
THE ILLNESS

1. Neil T. Anderson, *The Bondage Breaker* (Eugene, OR: Harvest House Publishers, 1997).

2. Joseph Thayer, *Thayer's Greek-English Lexicon of the New Testament* (Peabody, MA: Hendrickson Publishers, 1996 [reissue edition]), s.v. "*sarx*."

3. Gene Edwards, *The Divine Romance* (Wheaton, IL: Tyndale House Publishers, 1993).

CHAPTER 3
THE TREATMENT PLAN

1. Charles Spurgeon, *Holy Spirit Power* (New Kensington, PA: Whitaker House, 1996), 86.

2. Watchman Nee, *The Salvation of the Soul*, translation of original 1930 Chinese publication (New York: Christian Fellowship Publishers, Inc., 1978), 90.

Chapter 8
Subconscious Brain Functions—Programmed to Be Me

1. The Littauers' personality test can be obtained through CLASS Services Inc., P. O. Box 66810, Albuquerque, NM 87193, (800) 433-6633. Others can be found free online.

Chapter 10
Internal Rewards—Your Neurologic Motives

1. John B. West, MD, PhD, ed., *Best and Taylor's Physiologic Basis of Medical Practice*, 11th edition (Baltimore: Williams & Wilkins, 1985), 1273-1275.

Chapter 12
The Final Healing

1. Ewald Plass, *What Luther Says* (St. Louis, MO: Concordia Publishing House, 1959), 661.

2. Nee, *Salvation of the Soul*, 114.

Made in the USA
Middletown, DE
13 March 2022